What Kind of God?

An Attempt at Reconciling Human Experience
with a Seemingly Absentee Cosmic Landlord

Chris J. O'Loughlin

PublishAmerica
Baltimore

First printing

ISBN: 1-4241-5236-4
PUBLISHED BY PUBLISHAMERICA, LLLP
www.publishamerica.com
Baltimore

Printed in the United States of America

In eternally loving memory
of Lisa Ann O'Loughlin
My sister in flesh and in Spirit
No sibling could be more inspiring

Table of Contents

Chapter 1
Modern Times, Ancient Questions

Over the course of the days and weeks that followed the terrorist attacks of September 11th, 2001, as shock and anger began to give way to sorrow and reflection, people began asking themselves and others, especially their religious leaders, "What kind of God would allow such a thing to happen?" As a New Yorker, having witnessed the impact of the second hijacked plane into the south tower of the World Trade Center from three blocks away, I, too, would soon come to ask the same question. Thinking about the last moments and final seconds of the lives of the innocent working people in the upper floors of this living horror quickly turns reflection to anguish. And yet, of course it is nothing compared to the horror and agony those poor souls experienced before dying. Having been raised a Catholic, and always wanting to believe in a personal God, despite several periods in my life where I chose not to participate in the Church for various reasons, I struggled to reconcile belief in that God with this unbearable reality.

Indeed, for those who possess, but struggle with, their faith in God (from the perspective of *any* religion of conscience), it is a question that has thrust itself to the forefront of the collective consciousness and has become relevant to the times we live in for those who seek to make sense of the human experience. In fact, I don't think there's *anyone* who doesn't ask "What kind of God?" at some point in their lives, regardless of their cosmology. Atheists often ask it when defending their assertion that they see no evidence for the existence of God. The faithful struggle with the question because they want to believe that there is a God but such things thrust their faith into crisis. And agnostics ask it because they're undecided! It is indeed, a universal query.

In posing the "what kind of God" question to clergy and theological scholars, we may often hear a response similar to the following: It is *people* that perpetrate these things, not God that *allows* them, it is Man's inhumanity to Man. On an emotional level, and out of deeply felt compassion for what those poor people in the World Trade Center, the Pentagon and the hijacked airliners went through, we find it hard sometimes (the sensitive and reflective), to reconcile belief in what we cannot see with the experience of ourselves and others. I say this because that which we see with our own two eyes everyday in an early twenty-first century, is a world which seems to be going more insane with each passing day.

For us New Yorkers, and American citizens in general, the terrorist attacks brought home, literally and figuratively, this timeless question of the ages: How could there be a God that creates people capable of perpetrating such unthinkably murderous madness? For instance, let's take the holocaust for example. How did God sit, apparently idly by, as six million Jews were systematically annihilated? And indeed the question applies throughout history. Many have asked, "Where was God?" during the Bubonic plague of 14th century Europe, to name but one of many plagues which, over the span of only five years, killed twenty five million men, women and children— fully one *third* of the population of Europe. And in modern times, eight hundred thousand innocent lives were brutally taken in yet another attempt at genocide, this time in Rawanda,

Africa. Where was God? Earthquakes, tsunamis and hurricanes have devastated communities and whole cities and taken countless lives over the millennia. We know, painfully, that the list goes on, throughout recorded history.

We see people born healthy of mind and limb, and we see people born disabled for life, or people who develop mental illness, whose brain chemistry, becomes out of balance, causing their experience of the world to be a living hell. We see small children dying of cancer or rare diseases like Progeria (premature aging which causes the body of a small child, organs and all, to be identical to a person of advanced age). The crippled, the blind, the poor, the stricken and victims of war continue to shake us out of ourselves, forcing us to ask that most fundamental of questions: why?

What good could possibly come of such terrible suffering for tens of thousands of years? We ask this because we seek purpose and meaning, in an effort to understand the world around us, which would help us to get along in life. We ask this because human suffering comprises more than man's inhumanity to man, but includes a wide array of natural misfortune as well. We want so badly to understand "what it all means" and what our role in *it* is. Indeed we are hard pressed to define the meaning of "it" in this phrase. Is the *it* in "what it all means" the sum total of human experience? And if so, did God have a *grand design* plotted out from before the beginning of time as we know it—or is the story of *it* something that we humans participate in writing?

Are we pure cosmic accident? If we are *not* an accident, but are indeed the product of an ultimate creator, a "Supreme Being," then are we born with the book of our lives already written, end and all? Do we have no say in how the chapters are to be worded, let alone concluded? Are we all just cosmic puppets, with our destiny pre-ordained by what would effectively be a cosmic puppeteer, dancing out the irrevocably plotted out course of our life and death? Or do *we* get to choose what strings to pull?

Chapter 2
Choices

Let's take the "man's inhumanity to man" dilemma and analyze the idea of "free will." We like to believe that we decide what our process of cognition is, our thought apprehension and comprehension. We like to believe that when we choose a course of action (or inaction for that matter; as writer Neil Peart of the rock band Rush declares in his song "Free Will," if you choose *not* to decide, you *still* have made a *choice*), it is because we engaged in the intellectual activity of choice, not that we were pre-programmed to have *made* that choice, whatever it turns out to be, *a priori*. Although some people, on pretty good merit, argue that it can never be proven one way or the other. Most of us like to (choose to) believe that we are in the driver's seats of our lives (we just may not have the car of our dreams is all!).

But there are those who are of the school of thought that says "if there *is* a God, He/She/It *made* you to make the choices you make, because He knew, being the Supreme Being (omniscient and all), what those choices would be before you finally thought *you* arrived at them." This is an intellectual "hoop-jump" that seems to slam you into a wall. For me, it brings up another question: Why in the world (universe, dimension, whatever) would a Supreme Being (call it what you like) create a sentient species with adaptability, intelligence, ability to reason and the capacity for an intangible, ineffable emotion called love, simply for the purpose of watching some cosmic movie in which every character, everyone who was ever born, is hard wired to be either moral or immoral, able bodied or crippled, blind or sighted and watch them play out the pre-destined events of their lives on the screen of existence? When the credits roll, what true purpose will this imaginary cosmic movie have had? Aside from God giving himself the ultimate Oscar for best creator and director, what real and true *merit* will it all have had in the end? For my part, I can't see how such a scenario would have any merit at all.

Therefore, for the sake of argument, let's proceed with our analysis first from the idea that there is indeed an original cause, and second, from the idea that, although God is omniscient, that we are not fated to think and do everything that we think and do. I base this position on the idea that we, within the realm of limitation, who are finite, cannot dictate to the Ultimate Source, Limitlessness itself, what the nature of what It creates can or should be. Let's put it this way: When you're God, you can do whatever you want, including create people that choose how they are going to respond to their environment and to each other, for themselves. As far as God's ability to create life, yet at the same time give it its own independence, what can I say? That's why He's God: When you're the master of all time, space and dimension, to use the vernacular, *you just got it like that.*

Also, many of us (indeed many throughout history) long to believe in ultimate justice, in ultimate good and the idea that what is good and right will ultimately be set to proper balance to the satisfaction of all for all time. Now, granted, the definitions of "justice" and "good" have been struggled with since Plato wrote the words of Socrates of Athens some two and a half millennia ago and so have many great philosophers throughout the centuries. But for my purpose I'll refer to the idea of "good" (moral good) as understood to mean the opposite of intentional harm, wrong-doing or destruction (although it could be argued that what seems to us to be terrible, could have a part in the greater good of the accomplishment of human experience even though we, unable to see the forest for the trees, cannot apprehend it)—and ultimate justice to mean that those who did intentional harm will come to account in ultimate finality, and that all will be set to rights in transcendent finality. However, if we are to be held accountable for choosing actions that cause intentional harm, should we not, by the same sense of justice, be given credit for making choices that promote the greater good or advance good will? Now of course this comes down to the simple idea of reward and punishment. When we choose to avoid intentionally causing harm or destruction, do we do so solely out of fear of being punished for it in the afterlife? And conversely, when we choose to take action to promote the apparent "good," are we choosing so simply because we hope to be rewarded in some paradisiacal afterlife? What would the true merit and purpose be in being good little boys and girls if it were simply because we are scared of the big bad tyrant in the sky called God and his terrible wrath? What would the point be, in choosing *not* to harm or destroy, if it is only because we just can't wait for our share of a reward in the afterlife?

Therefore, for the idea of "good" to have any real meaning and ultimate merit, it seems to me to have to be a choice made of its own accord for no reason but benevolent freewill itself, with no reward in mind and no avoidance of punishment feared. This may be at the heart of the reason why God created people in the first place, so that good would hopefully prevail in the end *not* because it was hard wired from before time to do so, but that it does so of its own conscious merit, giving itself ultimate meaning and God and people ultimate affirmation, for ever having existed in the first place.

It is no new argument. The philosopher Emmanuel Kant outlined his system of behavioral ethics, which espouses the "good for its own sake" position, which is called "Deontology." However, there are those who subscribe to what I view as the opposite sentiment, put forth by philosophers of the Utilitarian discipline, such as John Mills, who held that ethical decisions must/needs be based upon achieving results which would, in practical everyday terms, benefit the most people. For example, to use a character from popular culture, fans of the *Star Trek* television series would agree that Dr. Spock would be a Utilitarian, as illustrated by his famous quote, "The good of the many outweigh the good of the few, or the one." Undoubtedly, there are situations in which Dr. Spock's logic (his forte) is sound. One popular example of this still seems to be the reasoning which asserts that dropping Atomic bombs over the Japanese cities of Hiroshima and Nagasaki in August of 1945, in order to end the Second World War and save many more lives than it ended, makes Utilitarian sense. But I will argue further that when seeking ultimate merit and purpose to human life, struggle and death, that choosing good for its own sake seems to more clearly illuminate the greater underlying meaning of moving through the human experience: Namely, affirmation of goodness and love out of freewill, and doing so for no reward or avoidance at all, but being its *own* reason.

Chapter 3
So What *Does* It All Mean?

We've all had those moments of quiet reflection where we find ourselves asking that fundamental, but timeless and most profound, of questions: Why was I, or for that matter, *anybody,* ever born? Who or what, if anything, created people, and to what end, and for what ultimate purpose? And all this suffering that people have endured throughout the ages, and still endure today, and all the atrocities that people perpetrate on one another, and natural disasters and disease, for goodness sake, to what end or purpose do we witness these things? So many people, in jest and in deadly earnest, have looked at me in moments ranging from those of joyful lighthearted conversation to ones of deepest despair and sorrow and simply asked, "What's it all mean?"

Could it all (the Universe, any dimension of existence, any thinking, feeling, beings) just be a cosmic accident, come into being by pure random chance and ultimately returning into absolute nothingness, leaving nothing permanent behind but the meaninglessness of having existed at all? Well, experience, reflection and a certain sense of the ineffable tell me resoundingly, *no*. It seems to me that human experience cannot have come into being by pure chance and that not only human life, but human suffering and even death, all have self affirming meaning and, indeed, are as they *must* be. I realize that this may seem a scandalous claim, but I will develop and support the idea on the pages that follow. All things are as they must be in order for existence and human experience to have meaning, merit, and affirmation. I will explain why I'm convinced, on several levels, that this is the case.

I am both painfully and joyfully aware that the great thinkers of the ages all have pondered and struggled with the big questions. I write under no pretense that existentialists and theologians throughout history with credentials far greater than mine haven't already put forth their theories on the meaning of human life. Many have humbly submitted that the question simply cannot be answered with absolute certainty. Indeed many suggest that nothing at all can be known with absolute certainty. I, of course would be arrogant to think that I can settle the matter, grappled with throughout time by the greatest minds that have ever lived, with the wave of a writer's wand. Nonetheless, the words of Socrates of Athens echo in my mind, heart and soul: The unexamined life is not worth living. The gadfly pesters us still (Socrates, because he pestered people with inquisitive demands for clarity, was called the gadfly), two and a half millennia later, and I'm sure he would have it no other way.

Chapter 4
Making a Case for God

Absence of evidence is not evidence of absence. This word play certainly applies to the God question. However, I would like to suggest that there is indeed evidence of the existence of a creative intelligence functioning as the impetus behind the beginning of all things. I'd like to proceed from the fact that there is sound scientific evidence that there *was* indeed a burst of matter and energy which began space and time as we know it. The question science *cannot* answer is, "what caused that great explosion of matter?" The law of cause and effect tells me that someone, thing or being, "lit the fuse" that ignited the Big Bang.

All of the galaxies man has ever discovered are all racing away from each other in all directions of space with staggering speed, indicating that they share a common starting point, namely the beginning of time and space as we know it. Such a conclusion is based on objective, empirical, scientific methodology. For a detailed explanation of why Big Bang theory is accepted as near certainty from a purely scientific perspective, I would refer the reader to contemporary scientific authorities who can articulate on matters of physics far better than I ever could: namely, Carl Sagan, author of *Cosmos*— Stephen Hawking, author of *The Universe in a Nutshell* and Brian Greene, author of *The Fabric of the Cosmos.*

For all the chaos out in the far reaches of space and here on Earth, there is far more order in the physicality of the universe than not. This is true despite the fact that the second law of thermodynamics states that any physical system naturally tends toward a state of lesser order, or higher *entropy*. Nonetheless, gravity alone, whatever that *really* is, provides an astounding feature of order and even symmetry to the way things are. From the orbits of subatomic particles like protons and electrons around their nuclei to the orbits of moons and planets, there is cohesion, there is consistency, there is *law*. Yes there is chaos, celestial bodies can be smashed for any number of reasons forming meteors and other cosmic debris which can cause cataclysmic collisions and there are anomalies in space like singularities (black holes), but even *they* come into being by the law of cause and effect. There are *rules* (the laws of physics): from the microcosmic to the macrocosmic, we see systematic consistency governing the way things are (with the exception of Quantum Theory). How could it be that not only all that exists but all that exists having a law book come into being by accident? How could an accident have led to you, reading this page right now with a sense called sight, as you effortlessly hold this book in your hands using the staggeringly complex network of nuero-pathways and electromagnetic impulses in your brain, to process information and ideas in the form of written symbols entering your cornea via complex processes involving light and the intricacies and dynamics of sight, to travel along nerve cells and somehow register in your consciousness as cognition? The staunchest atheist must admit that this would be a pretty mysterious accident.

And yet, the more scientists learn about the way things are and how the universe works, the more confounding the ever elusive idea of total comprehension of existence becomes. Quantum mechanics set the world of physics spinning on its head with its randomness and uncertainty as to the way particles in the realm of inner-space behave. This only suggests to me that there not only is a designer of all that is, but that this designer created a matrix for the physicality of everything, and then built into it mysterious properties, and, if you like, layers of reality, that make absolute understanding of that matrix a challenge that seems to have no end. And yet we (the products of pure happenstance in some cosmic burp?) continue to question the nature of what we perceive to be our existence by *accident?* Is Descartes' timeless assertion "I think, therefore I am" the product of absolute *nothingness?* Are we to understand that an art and architectural creating, music making, poetry writing, space faring species capable of altruistic acts of unconditional love is to be regarded as having plopped into being complete with a framework to *be* in, from *absolute* nothingness? Science itself would have to agree that if all that exists in the cosmos, is the ultimate effect, surely then there must be an ultimate, original, *cause*. But purely scientific endeavor stops (short) here and asserts that what cannot be experimented upon and verified by scientific method can only ever be mere abstract notion. Cleary then, to find purpose and meaning to human experience, science can and should *inform* our eventual conclusions, but cannot be and should not be the only criteria available to consciousness in the process of arriving at those conclusions.

People throughout the ages have sensed that there is some numinous reality that is responsible for all that is. Even in polytheistic cultures and periods of history when gods and goddesses were concepts used to explain things that both delighted and frightened people in nature but which could not be understood, there was the sense of the ineffable, the intangible, which led to the idea, or more accurately in my opinion, the realization, that there is a Supreme Being of some indefinable nature, behind the realm of physical existence, and of course this lead to all the religions of the world. The formal religions of the world, those which are monotheistic and those which do not feature a necessarily personal God (like Buddhism for example), deal with human suffering in different ways. I'd like to offer some ideas regarding suffering which may have been influenced by religion (Christianity in particular) but which conform to no particular religious dogma. For instance, the Catholic doctrine of "original sin" is not reconcilable to my sense of the nature of God, life, or suffering. So I had to turn to independent thought, tempered by intuition, in order to come to terms with the idea of a God who allows suffering; suffering resulting from both nature and human intention.

Chapter 5
The Necessity of a Dual Universe

Try to imagine a universe, an existence, a human experience, in which nothing had an opposite. I humbly submit, it is rather hard to do. It quickly becomes a slippery slope of frustrating thought because no idea or phenomenon can have any appreciative meaning, albeit in a relative sense, without comparison to that which is contradictory to it. What would the idea of "up" mean without a "down" to compare it to? (There is an idea in physics called "translational invariance," which asserts that there is no such thing as an absolute spatial orientation without the grounding of a fixed point of reference). So, in order to make sense of *anything*, even where one is in space, the concept of opposition is necessary.

Let's take the idea of "beauty," the idea of defining beauty even in an abstract sense. For instance, what is its *real* nature? In other words, not what visual, aural or emotional characteristics it has that are compelling and appealing, but what is the underlying *something* that gives rise to calling something beautiful, be it a person, thing or idea? When you arrive at your conclusion, whether your criteria are Socratic (inquisitive and analytic concerning that which may be *underlying*) or purely superficial—what gives merit to your perspective without considering the absence of what you consider to be *un-beautiful*? I suggest a simple thought experiment. Imagine a world in which *everyone* alive on Earth had physical features and characteristics that you consider to be beautiful; to a person, without exception. Let this world populated exclusively by beautiful people come into existence in your mind spontaneously, as if you are the God of a universe inside your head. Now let's fast forward time in this universe (you're God, you can do that). Let's say, a thousand years. Now jump ten thousand years, then go further and quantum leap to a million years, all without a single person, thing or idea that you consider to be un-beautiful. Do the people in your universe have any concept of what beauty is? How can they? How can they appreciate even the most abstract notion of what beauty is, in a universe that has no opposing principle to give it merit or meaning? Eventually, you may return from your reverie a little shaken up, but relieved to be back in a universe where things have an opposite to define them and give them merit and meaning.

Now let's attempt to deal with the question concerning the ultimate meaning of the word "good." Good natural phenomena, good will, good weather, and good experience: what would make them good without their opposites to compare them to? Now I must be clear that I do not intend to imply that evil is therefore necessary so go out and perpetrate wrongful acts of conduct; that would be missing the point entirely. But if *everything* and *everyone* were *all* good, *all* of the time because they were hardwired to *be* that way, where would the true meaning and merit of the idea of "good" ultimately lie? Let's return to our thought experiment in which you are the God of your own mental universe. You have made *everyone*, by their nature, and without ability to choose, a person of good intention. Everyone loves everyone else all the time and takes care of each other without fail or exception, not because they choose so, but because they have been hard-wired by their maker to know nothing else. What meaning would "the good" have if it were force fed by some cosmic tyrant of the warm and fuzzy? It would be Utopia. Fair enough (Utopia literally *means* "nowhere" by the way). But would the universe you created have any real merit? What would affirm the existence of this universe? It's not easy to be God is it?

So it seems that to give validity to the nature of existence, duality had to be "allowed" into the cosmic mix. And free will comes back into the conversation here, because the very idea of free will could not exist except in a universe of duality. Because, obviously, one has to have two opposites to choose from in order to exercise free will right?

There are those who believe that the dual nature of both the physicality of the universe and the duality inherent in humankind (everyone has some good and some bad) are a reflection, indeed a statement, that the nature of God Himself (Herself/Itself) must also be dual. You might hear someone say "If all are created by God, including torturers and murderers, then the origin of their behavior and evil will can be traced back to that which created them, therefore God himself must be half evil"—He made them didn't He? This is a sentiment I have heard argued while having debates concerning the nature or existence of free will. I must say that it cannot be denied that there is a certain amount of linear logic, an inductive reasoning which makes it appear that the equation is balanced and therefore final. However, if thought through thoroughly, one comes to realize that the equation is doomed to collapse. Because for human experience to have any meaning that truly affirms its existence, free will must be built in, and for free will itself to have any merit to its own existence, it *must* exist absolutely and utterly *independent* of God. Indeed, it places limitations on a Being of *infinite* capacity in its rather simplistic and reductive assertion that if evil exists, the creator must have some degree of evil as part of Its nature. If God is indeed infinite and beyond our ability to comprehend, how can we say that it is impossible for that God to create sentient intelligence that (with the exception of mental illness, where faulty and/or imbalanced brain chemistry makes the afflicted incapable of being responsible for their actions) is responsible for its own decision-making process? Again, what value would there be to free will if *any* aspect of it were manipulated or "programmed" before the fact, including whether each individual would tend toward either benevolent *or* harmful conduct? Indeed a certain kind of "divorce" from God had to take place (what I call the "first rift") in order for humankind to evolve and make choices that, in the end, can be fairly called our own.

Now is this to say that I personally am a proponent of Deism? It may sound that way but actually I am not. First, for those not familiar with the idea, Deism is a theory in theology which asserts that God created the universe and everyone and everything in it, set the world about its axis and started it spinning, and removed his hands altogether, sitting back and basically having nothing to do with it after that. No influence, no intervention, no participation whatsoever. Well, because of the necessary "divorce" I cited above, I do indeed believe that there was *one, single, solitary* exception to that idea. And as we know, one exception breaks the rule altogether. I will develop my idea as to why such an arrangement must and *had* to be the case in order for things to make sense in a relationship between humankind and God where such a divorce was necessary, but ultimately reconcilable, for the existence of *either* to be truly affirmed later in this book.

Whoops! Did I just commit the ultimate blasphemy and imply that God needs *anything* to affirm His (Her/Its) existence, let alone need *people!* How *dare* I?! Well, to be honest, I really don't think it's such an outlandish concept.

Let's return to our thought experiment mode, in which, by virtue of our imagination, we can think, we can do, and we can *be*—*anything* we want, all in the safety of the laboratory of the mind. Okay, suppose you are God okay? (Stay with me now and don't be afraid to think freely and never let *anyone* limit how you use your imagination, always remember, imagination has been the key to unlocking every insight ever experienced in any area of endeavor).

Alright, so there you are—God, in infinite splendor and glory, hanging out there in the timeless dimension of eternity, with no particular shape or form. Now mind you, I'm not asking you to imagine that you are the wise old sage archetype with a long white beard sitting on a throne upon a cloud, resplendent in a flowing white robe; but instead a sort of absolute supreme existence that simply IS. No angels because you don't need anybody right? And besides, angels are just intermediaries between God and people anyway right? And in *our* scenario, there is nothing in any form of existence except God. Just sort of radiating infinite light into…into…into what? What does light illuminate? It illuminates darkness right? Without a dual universe, there can be no darkness, and therefore, no meaning or purpose for the light. And of course we use the word "light" literally but also, metaphorically. This "light" that God radiates would, I have to think, believe, and feel, to be pure unmitigated, unconditional and perfect Love. Now, what reality or affirmation does love have without that love being *experienced*—being given and received? I think most of us recognize love as a feeling—an emotion so powerful it defies description or comprehension: Ineffable and sublime, it is the underlying and transcendent phenomenon that arguably, is God

Himself. It is a bond that can never be understood. People lay down their lives, sacrificing all, in the name of Love. Without being a "will to power" it is the most powerful or most potent energy in any dimension or in any form of existence.

Now I ask you, wouldn't all this be quite a tragic waste if you didn't have anyone to radiate that that light *to*, anyone to share this infinite love *with*? In a simple—and yes, I know, daring— word, wouldn't you, in our "you are God" thought experiment, despite all of your omniscience, omnipotence and omnipresence get, well, just a little bit bored? And dare I say further, lonely? Of course I realize loneliness is a human emotion and I probably have no business associating it with a Supreme Being. But silliness is fun and sometimes helps to make a point. I mean, there you are, just whistling a magical beautiful melody into the vacuum of absolute nothingness for no one to hear, just twiddling your all powerful thumbs, contemplating how infinitely wonderful you are. A creator with no created. See where I'm going with my silly sarcasm? We *had* to get *begotten!* You wouldn't want God to be the ultimate Tree that falls in the forest making no sound would you? And you wouldn't want, I'll wager, the overall totality of human experience to be the ultimate tree that falls in the forest making no sound either right?

Meaning and purpose; sentient life, which is not pre-programmed, scripted or choreographed, means absolutely everything (as far as I'm concerned) when it comes to the human experience. And there is just *way* too much experience of deep affect and mystery to that experience for it all to be an absolute accident.

Without purpose there is no meaning, without meaning there is no merit, without merit there is no inspiration, without inspiration there is no affirmation, without affirmation there is no love, without love there is no hope, without hope, there is no life. And where there is no life, we have come full circle: there is no purpose. I can't see how intelligent Atheists (and there are many) can reconcile to themselves the idea that they, their loved ones, and all they ever thought, did, felt, and shared, has meaning and purpose if it all came out of nothing for no reason and will all *return* to nothingness for no reason.

The idea that all of existence is an accident and all of human experience absolutely nothing more, in the end, than a mind-bogglingly complex system of matter, coalesced and congealed into what would accidentally turn out to be a phenomenon called electro-magnetism and operating in an accidentally evolved network of neurons we call a brain, is just too much accident for me to consider reasonable. Reason, thought, reflection, contemplation—how can all of these spontaneously pop out of nothingness? Most atheists are empiricists that have confidence in science and scientific method, and much to their credit. Such qualities are admirable and intelligent. I submit then that as stated previously, it is *science* that tells us that without cause there is *no* effect. The universe as a whole (the known and unknown universe), all of life in general and sentient life in particular, would be the ultimate *effect*. It is science that therefore *must* predict that there is, with a high degree of probability, an ultimate *cause*. It is true, science cannot explain that cause right now, but it also could not explain thunder until scientific discoveries were made and new insights had. It won't be insights as to physical phenomenon that may lead us to a better understanding of the nature of God and of the human experience, but insights may yet come nonetheless. Just because we can't comprehend something does not mean that something must or cannot exist. Many bright people assert: "There is simply no evidence of the existence of God, that's all." Look in the mirror, my astute and observant friend, and behold—your evidence.

Now despite my conviction in the existence of an original cause, I, like most people, still grapple desperately over the *nature* of that cause, because such horrible things happen in the world. We try to make sense of human suffering, like the experience of grief for instance, which is an anguish that many people find to be simply unbearable. Yet, it seems that to embrace and try to think through the most painful questions can be transformative for us. It's a catharsis which will hopefully help me, and hopefully help you as well, to come to terms with such sufferings and carry on—especially if you have ever lost a family member or loved one. And if you haven't lost anyone yet, you will. No one is exempt from grief. It is a matter of how we respond to it and how we cope with it which defines our character. I choose to attempt to flesh out my emotions in the hopes of perhaps understanding them a little bit better which, in turn, helps me to live in the day to day world.

A few paragraphs ago I mentioned the biblically toned word *begotten*. This forces me to address the question: Begotten *how?* It is the oldest debate in the world. Did we come into existence spontaneously as homo-sapiens or did life evolve over very many eons? The debate has recently become heated again as Intelligent Design theory goes head to head against the theory of Evolution. To be honest, at the end of the day, I find it to be a silly debate. Why *must* it be a matter of one *instead* of the other? Why can't Evolution *be* Intelligent Design *in action?* Why must the scientific approach to understanding the origin of humankind necessarily be absent of an original cause? And why, for goodness sake, must the faith based approach to the understanding of our origin be devoid of scientific insights gained by the observations of facts?

For the atheist, whether we plopped into existence "overnight" or over time is inconsequential, because the atheist believes it all was an accident anyway. But if you believe we were *not* an accident, whether we were created in seven days or seven hundred million years isn't the important question. Is there a supreme cause *behind it? That* is the question! I'm not having that silly argument about an incestuous family, an apple, a snake and a blame game in a garden. I recognize metaphor when I see it. Besides, my intelligence tells me that it is sensible to trust in science and the scientific method. Besides, I refuse to ignore the fossil record and all it clearly shows; including the bones of both Dinosaurs and pre-modern man, like Neanderthal.

What's challenging to me is the question of *why* there must have been a period of evolution in a God started universe? Creation stories are all well and good for religions and cultures and the wonderful dynamic of human collective psychology in the form of the many mythological systems which informed the lives of so many throughout the world and throughout history. But when thinking this through as an individual, and intelligently recognizing the proof in the fossil record that there *was* a Paleolithic period and earlier forms of life on Earth I am faced with a Creator which, with infinite genius and grace, wished to allow the universe and life to come into its own *on* its own. There was nothing *contrived* about the framework out of which human life eventually would arise. For things to be affirmed as having merit, they must be allowed to take their own course unforced. Otherwise, all is contrivance and therefore, a kind of lie. Evolution keeps God, well, honest.

Chapter 6
Evolving into What? *For* What?

For me, it's important to put things in historical context. Doing so provides a much more comprehensive framework in which to attempt to gain understanding of a person or a people, a thing or an idea. So I find myself reeling in imagination, my head swimming with images of people and their hardships and their loves and their lives down through the eons. So long before history began to be recorded, so much human experience, and so much pain and suffering. And if the naturally caused tragedies like infant mortality, the death of mothers during childbirth, disease, starvation, extreme weather and predators weren't enough, human beings decided to begin killing each other for a host of different reasons. Land, resources, fear and a will to power over others, these things I bet were the reasons for the most ancient hostilities between groups or tribes because those things still are reasons people kill each other today. So you can bet that human experience has been a long hard road to say the very least for people of benevolence and conscience down through the ages.

And now, coming back to the modern age, with all the technological breakthroughs since the industrial revolution, despite all our toys and gadgets, what do we have to *show* for evolving over all those eons? People are still basically the same. Human nature seems to be the one thing that doesn't evolve, or does so at such an indiscernible rate and on such a subtle level so as to be imperceptible. *Can* human nature evolve? Or does the popular phrase *"it is what it is"* apply here? Then again, perhaps we are indeed, quite early on in the course of human evolution after all. Maybe with growth over the generations to come, people will co-exist in a warless world, and never harm each other anymore but help each other. My conscience reminds me not to be naive though, and that I just described Utopia. Utopia literally means "nowhere." It seems such a state of human affairs on an ongoing global basis can never be.

Why won't God *make* it be so? Doesn't it seem right and just that a beneficent God should and therefore must, if we are to believe in God's existence, do so? Shouldn't things be set to rights for goodness sake already?! And it would be a Kingdom of God established here on Earth with *real* truth and *real* justice *really* for all! Why not? In my opinion it is because such a thing would be nothing short of an intrusion and a contrivance. Shouldn't the human race ultimately, collectively grow up and come into an enlightened state on our own? Wouldn't we rather look back and say it's been a long hard road but eventually human beings chose benevolence over hostility? And as far as those who have perpetrated atrocities on their fellow human beings throughout the ages, all we can do is hope that there is indeed a God, and that true justice, whether it takes the form of some kind of punishment or something that we can't comprehend, will be applied to make things right. Enforcing justice here in the world we live in, can only be a function of the rule of law, but it cannot change the hearts and minds of those who would perpetrate harm or homicide. Such a thing can never and must never be forcibly imposed by being hardwired into our nature. Let's go back into the mental laboratory and let another internal psycho-drama play out in our minds-eye as an imagination based, thought experiment.

Chapter 7
A Thought Exercise in Behavior Modification

Suppose there is a young person, let's say a teenager, whose enraged sense of moral indignation is ripe to be unleashed onto the world. This person can be of either sex; perhaps you can imagine *yourself* at the age of, let's say sixteen or so. It's a difficult period in ones life. Being a sensitive person, you just can't accept that people do horrible things to one another. But one day you're walking down the street, let's say you're going to school and you witness a purse snatching. In disbelief you stare agape in horror as the thief runs away, having struck his victim; she lay bleeding on the ground as the perpetrator gets away. You feel your blood pressure rise and you point at the scoundrel and yell "stop!" Suddenly, like a video tape put on pause, the mugger freezes in motion. You quickly realize that by the power of your thoughts, like some Ultra-Super Hero, you have psycho-kinetic mastery over people's motions and all their physical actions and psychic power over their minds as well.

You immediately realize that these stunning new powers are yours because in your anger you wished the guy who knocked that girl down and took her purse so violently to be spun around upside down like a top and thrown violently onto the sidewalk. And just as you have this thought it *happens*. You wish him intense pain and he instantly writhes in agony. As you approach him you make it clear that it is indeed you causing him these punishments as you loudly announce the strange way in which he is about to be whipped about and slammed onto the pavement. Presently the crook begs for reprieve from the ordeal, and vows life long allegiance and obedience if only the punishment would stop. With a searing pain of warning shooting through his brain, you admonish the mugger that anytime he so much as has a violent *thought* his body and brain will be wracked with spasms of excruciating and burning pain. You give him a five second sample and he screams a blood curdling, deafening scream.

Now of course this whole scene would've played out in front of a crowd of curious onlookers who happen to be at the same intersection at the time of this supernatural punishment. But the crowd grows larger and larger within the minute or two it takes the drama to play out. In the crowd a newspaper reporter captures the whole thing on video tape. By six o'clock that evening you are known as "The Real Life Superhero" by millions of people worldwide.

After only a week of having people treat you in a suspiciously nice way such as never before and adversaries at your workplace bringing you donuts and coffee, suddenly you get a call from the FBI. It seems your services would be needed to foil a terrorist plot about to be executed beginning at a major airport. As you arrive you are greeted by special agents and scurried aboard a jetliner bound for a distant U.S. city.

Once onboard the terror suspects are pointed out to you by FBI agents. Quietly, you wait and observe the situation.

Before long the terrorists announce that they have a bomb and that nobody should move if they want to live. They begin to make their first moves toward the cockpit. You get up and follow them. The flight attendants expressions instantly morph from impatience and annoyance to dismay and then shock and horror as the terrorists come at them with previously hidden, makeshift weapons. With horrific visions of 9/11 in your head, your blood pressure rises and you lose your temper on the would-be mass murderers as you divert them away from the flight attendants and into the back of the plane where you freeze them upside down with your psychokinetic powers and inflict pain on them the likes of which they never imagined in their sickest dreams. You use your psychic powers to forcibly draw out of their minds the other flights and conspirators that would be involved in this new plot of mass murder.

As a result of your powers, and the information you force from the plotters minds, the entire plan is foiled and you are hailed as the major American hero of modern times. You are immediately approached by all branches of the armed forces and offered millions of dollars to participate in military activities. They are all harshly rebuked and made to suffer the pain of thousands of razor blades for even thinking of using your powers for their own agendas. The word spreads like wildfire that you can detect any person's ill intentions before the fact with your extra-sensory perception and torture them with unseen dispatches of punishing agony

Before very long, because word of such a person with such powers spreads like wildfire, people in the most remote, undeveloped and unspoiled, obscure corners of the world know of and fear you. Scarcely a living soul on planet Earth dares have a violent or immoral thought. Terrorists don't plot terror because they've seen the punishment inflicted by you on those with such thoughts detected going through their heads. And *acts* of violence? They just don't occur *anywhere* anymore. No one comes near you for fear that an impure thought might slip, uninvited to invade even their subconscious and unconscious minds. The world is at peace, and nobody harms anybody else. But you are alone because you are feared, not loved.

Now, do you feel like shaking your head and rubbing your eyes and bailing out of this experimental fantasy? I don't blame you.

So, what do you think of our world and who and what it contains as it existed in your mental movie? It must have felt pretty good to stop people from being able to harm and kill others. How did you fare with your newfound all-powerful abilities? Cruelty on Earth has actually *ceased* because of *you*. That's a *good* thing right? Of course it *should* automatically be a *good* thing because world peace must be one of the most exalted accomplishments the human race can ever achieve, right?

But shouldn't this force fed peace be something born out of natural course? If people cease to abuse one another but the reason they do so is because of fear of punishment, what merit is there in it? Actually, in my opinion only the perfect *opposite* of that scenario can truly represent the ultimate reconciliation between pure love, in omnipotent form, and ill will promoted by hatred and fear and the offspring of those things, which are ignorance and violence. But that's another chapter.

Therefore, if there *is* a God, wouldn't it make sense that how we humans behave would have to be left to *us?* Now I realize that accepting this is a harsh pill to swallow because it suggests that God stands by and lets human rights atrocities and natural tragedies occur as if He/She/It where an indifferent onlooker. The old question comes up again. "What kind of God would exist in such a way?"

Faith is the old answer. Faith gets many people through life and that's great. But after accepting the fact that to even believe God exists at all in the first place is a great leap of faith, as to His/Her/Its nature and our relation to it, I think the question begs analysis. My thought game about the omnipotent teenage mega-superhero is, of course, just another way to talk about free will. *True free will, not an illusion of it, is all important for the sum total of human experience to ultimately have self-affirming meaning.*

So then, what *really* gives existence its substantive meaning even when we acknowledge that free will is the only way to true merit and true merit the only way to true affirmation? Does anything else give us a glimmer of insight into hopefully higher purpose to human suffering in the broader sense? In other words, if my scenario of a world in which free will, of it's own natural human course, found itself evolved to a point of enlightenment where people everywhere lived in peace and according to the Golden Rule, there would still be much suffering and sorrow in the human experience. There is disease in nature. And when disease is fully eradicated from the Earth (good luck), a person can still slip and fall on a hiking outing, or be subject to disaster in maritime, aviation or ground traffic catastrophes. And any of these, of course, can lead to separating us from loved ones and family members. People would still suffer the physical pain of injury and tragic death and the agony of bereavement will be with us for the entire time that there is a human experience at all: anywhere.

My thoughts lead me to a question. "How would what's inside us that animates us and makes us individuals (in a God-created universe, let's call it the soul, in the Platonic sense, that which is born of the absolute, permanent and unchanging world of forms and ideas) *grow* or *evolve* into an entity that really, experientially *knows* what it's like to feel compassion or higher consciousness and truly meritorious existence without having gone through the archetypal heroes' journey: the journey of descent into the darkness, into struggling and through hardship and ultimately into triumph without having suffered hardship?" While growing up, I remember hating to hear the old adage: "through pain we grow." Until through years of living life, I found, through experience, a less corny way of framing the same sentiment: "what doesn't kill you, makes you stronger." This I found to resonate with me deep down inside, because the years had shown me so. I learned later, in reading some philosophy heavy-weights during my evening undergraduate studies, that this was a sentiment expressed by the challenging 19th century German philosopher Friedrich Nietzsche.

So what if there where nothing to challenge the soul to grow? What if the Supreme Original Cause Of Existence (provided there is indeed one, and provided there is a soul and not only temporary bio-chemical reactions at the center and essence of our awareness of ourselves and the world around us), set up a universe in which nobody can get sick or hurt, in which nobody has to plant a seed and hope for rain in order to eat, in which everyone is always comfortable right down to every step of terrain providing for comfortable walking, and in which there was no death and thus no bereavement? As tough as it is to write, it seems to me such a scenario would be a contrivance and therefore an illusion and no merited growth or affirmation of the soul could be shown to be truly *real* in this scenario. Mind you, I'm not crazy about the current arrangement of reality myself, I hate pain and bereavement. Physical, mental and emotional pain are all harsh and I wish we could do away with it all once and for all and maybe someday we will. But right now they are realities, so why not try to glean what insight we may in order to get us through the day?

Chapter 8
The Pain of Loss and Tragedy

It is, I think, a reflection of our individual and often collective placing of such high value on the potential of positive and affirming human experience during our fleeting visit through this fragile form that indeed informs and fuels our vehement dismay, sadness and even rage, when beautiful potential for affirmation of life is shockingly, tragically taken away from us. We instinctively want to lash out at the universe as part of the bereavement process, even to lash out at God, whatever our individual sense of that word is. Anger is a natural part of internalizing an unacceptable reality. If there can indeed be a healing along the road of this bereavement process; acceptance, I think, would be the beginning of it.

Before acceptance though, we (many of us anyway) feel betrayed by our idea of God. In our (at the time) desperately troubled minds and hearts we feel as though God has sentenced us (and our now departed loved ones), to the living out of a real-time nightmare. Our question returns: What kind of God would've put my loved one through such an ordeal and death? I know this from experience and so it may be worthwhile, both for the sake of sharing and of catharsis to add it to our inquiry into the nature of whatever God is and the human experience.

I'm referring to the loss of my younger sister, Lisa O'Loughlin. What she and my family went through, very many families go through different versions of, but for us, it was the worst case scenario because out of the three children in our family, either of her two brothers would've gladly traded places with her in order for her to enjoy the healthy, long and wonderful life she so richly deserved.

We grew up in a one parent household due to the effects of alcoholism inherited by our father, who, during the early years of being in recovery, participated in our upbringing as a weekend parent. Our mom put forth the effort of a saint despite her full plate and all through our childhood, it looked as though all three of us were relatively normal (my own academic mediocrity in elementary school not withstanding!) and on the way to pretty regular lives. Unfortunately though, our mom's side of the gene equation had a tendency for mental illness to arise. So the double helix of DNA would be a slippery slide for us three kids. Coming from either side we had potential for alcoholism, diabetes, Schizophrenia, or high blood pressure: It was practically genetic Russian roulette.

Chapter 9
"Fanny Farkle"

Lisa (my brother Greg called her "Fanny," short for Fanny Farkle, a 1960's television show character) was life-affirming potential personified. She encapsulated the hopes and dreams of what was, after all, a broken home. As she neared high school her radiant personal beauty resulted in a foray into modeling. Eventually she wound up on the cover of a hair care product much to the delight of us all. She had an abnormally advanced, prodigious intelligence, and rapidly became an over achiever in high school. A casual explanation of Einstein's theory of general *or* special relativity would be matter-of-factly offered during one of our encounters at the kitchen table while she took a break for a snack during a study marathon. She became enamored of American law and intended to pursue that passion while participating in mock trials at J.F.K. high school in the Bronx. She displayed a comprehensive understanding of the Constitution and was so adept at debate that despite being three years her senior, I stood no chance during any kind of verbal stand-off with her. And yet for all these talents and gifts, it is the *person* she was which was the most inspiring. She radiated with conviction that *nothing* good was impossible. The sheer tenacity of her spirit made her will indefatigable. Her character dictated going for the gusto and making a contribution out there.

And everybody loved her: And with good reason. She absolutely inspired you to not get down on yourself, and get up off your ass and be all you can be. A person just couldn't hope for a better family member. To say her future looked bright would've seemed an obvious understatement. It was clear that the sky was the limit for this remarkable young girl.

Our question is soon to raise it's inquisitive but befuddled head once more. During her sixteenth year, Lisa began to speak and behave in a manner consistent with one having a nervous and/or psychotic breakdown. We thought the self imposed rigors of over achievement had taken their toll and that an intervention was necessary. However, much to our horror it was far worse. Lisa gradually developed the symptoms of Schizophrenia.

Schizophrenia is one of the single most commonly and popularly misunderstood words in the English language. It does not mean she displayed different personalities or what used to be called Split-Personality and is now called Dissociative Identity Disorder. The prefix "schizo" or the "schism" in Schizophrenia is a split from objective perceptual reality and the brains ability to process that reality as coherent experience. Basically, A Schizophrenic is out of touch with reality. The brain and the processing of the five senses are broken. There are biological chemicals in the brain called neurotransmitters that act as data messengers along the nerve cell route or neuro-pathways of the brain. Each neurotransmitter must be present in a specific quantity and must not pass over the space between nerve endings, or synapses, in either too much or too little amount. In the case of Schizophrenia, It's Serotonin we are chiefly concerned with. (It's one of the things I am amazed most about in human beings. We are so delicately tuned to perceive and interact with, our environment. The complexity of the brain, I'm sure, will always be staggering). Serotonin is associated with lucidity among other things, like mood for instance. Also, when one has Schizophrenia both visual and auditory hallucinations may occur. In other words, the afflicted person may see and hear things which aren't there. One can be very out of sorts if there is an upset in the balance where Serotonin is concerned. And when severe, and that "broken brain" condition I referred to before, results in a mental illness, the word we commonly use in popular language is "crazy."

Faced with the profound severity of Lisa's illness, institutionalization was our family's only alternative. And unless the victim's family is wealthy, you'll find that our society has placed a low value priority on caring for the mentally ill. Local and State facilities are understaffed, conditions are poor and often unsanitary. When visiting my innocent baby sister I was often overcome with a terrible dread as if visiting an inmate at a correctional facility, not a patient at a hospital. However, these inadequate arrangements were now part of our reality, and Lisa's whole world. For even when she was relatively lucid as a result of the developing antipsychotic drugs of the late 1980s, she would be an "inmate" of an institution, deprived of liberty and autonomy. And I'm sure that even when you have the wherewithal to acknowledge that you have an illness which makes you potentially dangerous to yourself and others, you still have a problem with being imprisoned.

Lisa, as a small cog in a giant State wheel, was repeatedly transferred from one location to another as months turned into years and her condition remained unimproved. I was actually afraid to imagine what living *her* life inside *her* mind must've been like. There must've been the constant danger of violent patients and unpredictably violent outbursts. It's also horrifying to think of her *internal* experience of this living nightmare.

This was a mind capable of pondering the great mysteries of the universe, both scientifically and philosophically. I use the word "mind" here as different from the brain which, I believe, is the necessarily complex *housing* of the mind, but as being something which transcends the temporal. That mind, was effectively trapped in a housing which had gone haywire. Such a prodigious intellect and a sensitivity and generosity of spirit now in a distorted and surreal experience of the world; it was and remains hellish to even seriously contemplate. And would, of course also be so, as regards any person of conscience so afflicted. I must say though, and again to her credit, that when she was able to be in relative control of herself, when the medications worked at least to the point of keeping the voices and visual hallucinations at bay, she was mostly cheerful during the visits. She had clearly established a benevolent and genuine rapport with several of her fellow patients. It was the true Lisa shining through despite the illness and the conditions of institutionalized living.

For three years, from the ages of sixteen to just shy of twenty, she was transferred from location to location in the New York network of state facilities for the mentally ill. But on October 26th, 1987, Lisa somehow made her way to White Plains New York without fellow patients and without supervision. She made her way to a commuter railway station and by all witness accounts, jumped onto the tracks in front of an oncoming train. Whether schizophrenia or something of her true self that could stand it no longer was responsible for her action, we will never know, nor does it really matter. My hope is that in an instant no longer in duration than the blink of an eye, her suffering on Earth was over.

All of us in all the human community, have or will lose a family member; it comes of course with the turf of being mortal. Death is indeed part of life. For the faithful, in the abstract, death is thought of as a door to a new beginning. But only in an existence that is non-accidental and in which an eternal life source underlies all that is temporal. For those who perceive existence through purely Cartesian eyes (requiring empirical proof for the existence of anything that can't be measured and verified experientially), who mock and deride such faith as fanciful and as being the last resort of simpletons who believe in what I have often heard referred to as the "invisible man in the sky," when one of their family members dies, they cease to exist in a very absolute and final way. The closest to metaphysical they get is to say that the departed lives on in our memory. Living on through the memory of loved ones is no doubt a priceless *form* of immortality, but never was my need to believe in the immortality of the soul more urgently and desperately confronted as when we lost Lisa. I needed (and need) to believe *in a concrete and real-time* way that Lisa's soul lives on.

Belief in God, having, as I mentioned, been raised catholic, was tried from time to time for me as it is for anybody, as I was growing up, but was always in the abstract, not in the solid reality sense. I had been, to be objective and honest, indoctrinated into the Roman Catholic faith from early childhood, but as soon as I was old enough (although still a kid) I summarily rejected all I had been force fed about religion, like a normal healthy, authority questioning teenager should. Anyone who blindly and passively assumes the roles and faiths dictated to them by those who insist that they know better are, in my view, weak of mind, as well as spirit and character. Take up any religion of benevolence and conscience or throw it all away as hogwash but whatever you do, for the love of all humanity and dignity, do it out of a choice made by none other than *yourself*; combining thoughts and experiences from your entire life up to that time. And do yourself a favor; be open to your view possibly changing: not to do so would be like a tree that refuses water and sunlight. It would contort and distort under the natural influences of growth. And I say that as it applies either way, looked at from the perspective of a God*less* to a God-*started* universe. In this book I want to flesh out in writing *my own* process in this regard, and although it obviously has a bent toward the God-*started* universe, it is not my intention to convince anyone I may be lucky enough to have read this of the existence of God, but I would indeed, to be honest, be highly gratified to have prompted a person or two to think over the ideas I am trying to share.

The grieving process usually consists of several phases, including shock, denial, rage and acceptance. Dealing with the sudden and tragic loss of a loved one is absolutely universal whether there is any such thing as something that started all that is or not. For some, God is a part of their process, for others, not. I'm sure atheists grieve. They are thinking and feeling human beings. But I almost envy the cut and dry, black and white way about which the atheist would feel for their loss without the complication of the God issues and questions. It will never cease to be soul wrenching to my very core when I see a bereaved mother wailing, racked with sobs and repeating the agonizing question over and over "why God?" It's a heartbreaking faith to witness as well. That woman, in her deepest anguish, still *believes* in God. This is where the empiricist might have a strong argument for God being a manmade construct, perhaps a cognitive psychologist for instance. They may say that this construct is used as a crutch, or in a less derogatory way, a defense mechanism and is a function of denial. "Your loved one is gone, accept and move on" may be their advice. But for someone as emotional as I am, who feels that humans are infinitely priceless, especially loved ones, it is impossible to accept that someone so special and filled with love (a big topic in the God analysis, to be tackled later) simply ceases to exist in the most absolute sense. How can it be that the energy that would've housed and animated this person you knew, the internal experience of life, what they call the "phenomenological" self in psychology, all the emotions, thought processes, creativity, ability to make others laugh or cry, memories, hopes and dreams, and love for others simply cease to exist because the biological body was killed?

And yet in a God-universe, what are we to do with our relationship with God in order to reconcile belief? I say this because I know that those who have experienced bereavement don't always find it as easy to still believe as the mother I previously described, or this case specifically, my own mom. Many, especially when the tragedy occurred in the commission of a horrible act of violence or terror as in 9/11, refuse to believe anymore. I remember a woman from a PBS documentary called *Faith and God at Ground Zero* who denounced her belief in God openly. She had lost her husband and the depth of her grief and her willingness to share it tore me to pieces. I felt I *understood* why she would denounce her belief in God: Anger. No; not simply anger, that sounds like an insulting over simplification; more like unmitigated rage of the soul. They say we must process it and put it behind us, but boy do I understand her rage.

Chapter 10
The Morning I "Called God Out"

In the predawn hours of October 27th 1987, I was awoken by the sound of voices in the kitchen area of my Bronx apartment. One of them belonged to my room-mate and band member Ritchie. This alone wouldn't have been peculiar as Ritchie was an earlier riser than I. What *would've* been peculiar was the other voice. It belonged to my father. Growing up, the three kids in my family saw our father on weekends as my parents had been separated since before I was old enough to be aware. And by now my dad had long since remarried and I saw him on occasion. But it was around five o'clock in the morning on a weekday of a typical work week. To get a telephone call at that hour is almost never good news; to get a visit in person just *can't* be good. It's very hard to describe the very surreal state of mind this immediately put me in. Because before I had any real idea of what was about to be revealed to me a panic stricken dread came over me.

Lisa had gone missing on an outing with a group of her peers and a staff member of the facility she was residing in at the time, the day previous. I'll be honest; the following seconds were so emotionally traumatic that although I probably should remember my first exact words upon greeting my father, I don't. I know it was close to, if not exactly, "they found Lisa right?" There would be no "hello," "good morning," or "what's up, Dad, why ya here so early?" What I saw next I had never seen before in my life; my father's eyes began to well up. And I heard him speak through a choked voice for the first time in my life: "She passed away."

He had been silent as I approached him, not saying anything until I was close enough to embrace (or was it to hold back?) because after one of those nervous laughs of denial, wishing my dad was playing an over the top prank, which he was not the type for anyway, and as he began to weep openly, it came over me. Not a wave of sobs but a rage, the likes of which I had never imagined myself capable of, exploded within me. If grief could be a demon, it had just possessed me, because only Exorcists would've heard the language I was about to use.

I have never before or since been so overwhelmed with such an ineffable, agonizing urgency in the form of a raging demand by my spirit to leap out of my body. I cocked my head back, as if facing upwards, my father already holding back my immediate attempts to get away, and let out a loud, piercing scream. It's blurry but I remember these loud primal, guttural yells at the top of my lungs that soon gave way to the word "NO!" My fists where raging upward as I began giving my poor dad quite a hard time of holding me back; from where, I don't know.

The truth is Lisa and I had agreed upon a pact in childhood. We loved each other dearly and had long since pledged that the one wouldn't want to stay in the world without the other. My now uncontrolled rage filled me with the desire to run into my room. Maybe, I hoped in my panic, that I'll just run into my room and jump out the window to join her, and be true to my word. Maybe my dad knew that in my delirious state of rage that I might have been capable of hurting myself so I wasn't afforded the opportunity, without the burden of reflection, to just act. So I began to fight harder. I was wailing at the nearest wall with my fist in repeated, violent blows that damaged a plaster wall, something I wouldn't normally have been capable of. While this violent scene escalates physically, so do my words *and* my emotions *"towards God."* I cursed viciously in a way I'm not proud of but feel it's pertinent to share. Things to the effect of: "you mother fucker you! You had to take her didn't you, you fucking tyrant!" I howled with a maddened rage. Blow after blow, the worst names, I confess, that I had in my Bronx bred, street curse word vocabulary, I hurled up to God. And punch after punch, I put my adrenaline racked body into each swing at the wall. My truck driver father just kept his head down and arms locked around me, the old boy just wouldn't let go.

Soon, of course, I collapsed into sobs. I immediately began to flash back to our days in childhood as playmates. We fought like cats and dogs, as kids are prone to do, but I was, I guess in an attempt to comfort myself with comforting images, remembering how very exceptionally adorable she was as a little girl, and the way, even then, that we cracked each other up because even as little ones we knew what the other one was thinking, and would complete each other's sentences.

But getting back to my rage; I think there was something central to the God question in it. In fact I know there was. Amid my cursing and violent flailing, there was a question which was absolutely fueling the flames present there throughout the fit, whether I tried to word it out loud amongst my cursing I can't remember, but it was there nonetheless. It was this: "Can you— (God), in all your omniscience, really know, *really experientially KNOW*, what this hell is like? To lose the flesh and blood spirit kin you loved so very, very deeply." This desperate, living emotional hell, I demanded that God know what it's like, *on the human side of eternity.* "You can't know what it's like," I asserted, "because you have not *been* here!"

However, in those first hours and days of bereavement, because it was love and affection that kept me and my family from literally going insane from grief, (and I still felt that those things emanated from a God based universe), and because grace seemed to be present in every family member's embrace and every friend's embrace, that I chose to surrender to a feeling of closeness to God. Not because I had such great insights or was such an unshakable believer because neither of those thing are true, but because *despite* myself, something called grace, an ineffable quality of divinity, that soothes and reassures and is patient and is of unconditional love wrapped me in Its embrace and kept me going. I think it's available to, and keeps all good people, going. Many would say it is nothing more than the effects of bio-chemicals brought on by being hugged every couple of minutes in your hours of distress. I'd would only half disagree. I don't deny the bio-chemical power of the human touch. It's just that there is a *sense* to it all which from *my* experience undoubtedly *transcends* bio-chemistry as it is *of* something that positively *underlies* it: The fact that we are animated of something extra-accidental. Having lost Lisa reinforced my belief in God as it is the only scenario in which her consciousness goes on existing, her life essence; her soul.

Chapter 11
The Question of the
Seemingly Absentee Cosmic Landlord

Straight to the center and essence of the nature and "personality" of God and the meaning of human experience in the universal sense is where my demand of God led me during my fit of bereavement and consequential hours of calmer reflection. As discussed earlier, there had to be a duality based universe in order for there to be legitimate affirmation of the human experience. Free will was an absolute must for the meritorious confirmation of goodness. For what meaning would it (goodness) have without its absence in the world? What about compassion then? How could this seemingly divinely inspired emotion exist without suffering? ("com" means "with" and "passion" means "suffering.") And as for love, if it were forced upon us it would have no meaning, no merit, no affirmation of its own.

But that still doesn't satisfactorily answer my question: What kind of God would just leave us to work out the rift caused by duality on our own, just setting things in evolutionary motion and staying out of the picture? This is the scenario in a cosmogony known as Deism, hence my sarcastic quip about the absentee cosmic landlord. Because if this condition of mortality, opposites, and suffering is crucial to the affirmation of good will and love having absolute meaning of their own accord, it would seem rather cruel for the "Landlord" to leave Himself/Herself/Itself out of the struggle; a kind of trans-dimensional tyranny if you like. What would set things right?

What could close the rift? What could prove, while leaving the mechanism of the cosmos as they are and as they must be, left to their own natural devices, and without tampering with free will, leaving, as must be done, those who choose, with their free will to ignore goodness, compassion and love, to act out their opposition to good will, so as not to play puppet master with the universe or the human race and yet, at the same time, be the ultimate act of perfect love?

I will make the case that love is the reason for all existence. When people ask you "what is the meaning of life?" I'm confident that the short answer is the central and all encompassing answer: Love. Now, of course I'm offering this argument for those who entertain the notion of a God based universe but just can't reconcile to reason, or emotion for that matter, the seemingly insurmountable hurdles posed by suffering, bereavement and death.

For those people convinced that they are living in an accident based universe, I hope you continue reading as I don't intend to preach but for you, love is a chemical reaction that ultimately originates in absolute nothingness and will return to absolute nothingness. For me, love is the only thing that ultimately gives meaning and purpose to the entire spectrum of human experience and perfectly justifies what seems to me to be the One divine intervention in the human story.

Now, mind you, I said it "seems" that the Landlord is absent, but I didn't say that I believe this to be absolutely the case.

So, not only to close the rift and set things to rights, but for my question to be answered on *this side of eternity* and for us to be shown that indeed, here in this fragile form, God does indeed know what it is like to experience pain, doubt, fear, suffering, bereavement and death. There had to be a participation; a sharing in the human form. It makes sense. Therefore I believe the following: That even though there *may* be life elsewhere in the universe, and I will address that question, God chose to participate in the human experience by way of personification here on Earth in the person of Jesus of Nazareth.

Now, religiosity can get in the way of religion, and both can get in the way of objective, philosophical contemplation of the nature of God and the human experience. Having formalities and instruction heaped upon you in the form of dogma that is deemed "infallible" sometimes short-circuits one's ability to think things through for themselves, and form a connection or "link" to their own sense of what the numinous is and what religious experience is. (The very word "religion" comes to us from a Latin word that translates to "linking back.")

Fundamentalist religiosity has directly led to things like the Crusades and the Inquisition. And also indirectly led to the Nazi Holocaust (remember, Hitler thought himself a "Christian" and partly used his twisted misconception of Christianity to justify the holocaust of six million Jews and millions of Christians of the "wrong" sect of Christianity). These things were unqualifiedly horrible and positively antithetical to the act of perfect love and reconciliation that I'm referring to. Religiosity also tends to negate the validity and legitimacy of other cosmogonies and cosmologies. All of the religions of benevolence and conscience in the world, major and obscure alike, are paths to God if indeed we are living in a God based existence. I have personally "linked-back" to Christianity because, after being indoctrinated involuntarily as a child into Catholicism (which means *universal* and ought to start living up to it), but later, in early adulthood, rejecting the formalities of the religion, I have come, over time, having suffered much emotional agony and deepest reflection, to believing in The Incarnation through my own thoughts and feelings. I find that it is what I always come back to in times of most desperate despair and even anger at God because of the suffering here on Earth.

Chapter 12
What Kind?
More Loving Than We Can Imagine but
Probably Tougher Than We Would Prefer

Yet, inevitably I come full circle, face to face with my own convictions about God not playing puppet master with the universe and everyone in it. And yet, indeed *not* being an absentee landlord as Jesus demonstrated because now I'm face to face with a God who isn't afraid to get his hands dirty, and not to mention, much, much worse. And so, again, when faith is tempered with *reason*, religiosity need not get in the way with formalities and demands.

For me, the "what kind of God?" question is answered if it is true that Jesus is the personification of God. And so now, whenever I shake my fist at God and, through gritted teeth, demand to know "do you know what this suffering is like?" the suffering that comes par the course of human living? The answer I can imagine to come from God is "yes, I do." In a scenario (of faith) in which there *is* a God who created all of existence but had to *let things be* of their own accord and merits, this belief provides a way to close the rift created both by my question of "do You (God) *really* know what it's like?" Also, it closes the rift created by the choice arrived at, through free will by many, to be selfish, greedy, cruel and murderous.

How? Because in a universe in which God participates in humanity, God would know what it's like to be human and lose someone you love to death or tragedy or brutality. God would be *empathic*, not just omniscient and transcendent. It is for the sake of unconditional, perfect love for humanity that God, I believe, chose to be *immanent* and accessible: A participant, not an absentee Landlord in the human story. It makes sense because it allows for free will and evolution but doesn't, like I heard a freethinking priest once put it while studying a Theology course at Fordham University "let God off the hook" (William O'Malley S.J.). The true sense of the phrase here, of course, is to refer to God not letting *Himself* off the hook. And that, to me, speaks of a God that is Love itself.

Chapter 13
A Contradictory Concept?

How could the Infinite, be finite? How can God and man be one and the same? Good question: especially since we know that humans are imperfect and believe (those who believe in a God-based universe) God to be perfection itself. Aren't the two, irreconcilable? Actually I think that's exactly the point. The two *are* reconciled by this miracle (and believe me, I acknowledge this to be a point of *faith,* only *complimented* by reason) which *had* to happen in order to close the rift. So the perennial question of "what kind of God would allow such suffering and death?" is answered for all times by a God that would've had to have, by virtue of living a life as a human, no doubt, experienced illness, experienced doubt and sorrow (because, in the finite form he might have been aware of his identity but to be also truly human would've experienced the base human emotions) as well as the experience of the joy of love of family and friends. Also, he would've experienced the agony of seeing and feeling human suffering: God in spirit, human in flesh.

The common metaphor for this has classically been "the Son of God." But God doesn't have children the biological way that *we* have children of course, even though Jesus had to come into the world through a biological mother. I think of it this way: The infinite spirit that animates all of existence continues to exist in it's infinitude perennially, transcendent of time and space, but that through which *all life emanates and manifests*, the Christ, was conceived in the womb of mother Mary, to be born human, even while, uninterrupted, the omnipresent spirit of God *continues* to exist as the creator and master all dimensions. And a third "person," if you like, would be the "Soul" that inhabits the incarnation on Earth. A human body born your standard way, but animated by a spirit one and the same with God: A *Holy* Spirit. This is how I come to terms with the abstract concept of the Holy Trinity.

Why a trinity? It seems to me that God can choose to manifest himself in more ways than one and still be truly One. I don't know, but it *does* seem to me revelatory that some of the most fundamental phenomenon in existence come, in *three's*. For instance, the dimensions in which the universe exists: Time and space are the first two examples, and they are so entwined so as to be really one overall schema as the framework for the universe to exist in. Time, in its most basic definition is the 1) *past*, 2)*present* and 3)*future*. Space is *1) up 2) down, and 3)sideways*, or 1)*height*, 2)*width* and 3)*depth*. Another good one is *1) Man 2) Woman and 3) child*. Also, the human gestation period is three times three months. And then there's possibly my favorite; the fact that *three* notes are required to build a *chord* in music: Three notes in harmony together make a whole which is greater than the sum of its parts. And then, finally, If I may *stretch* the metaphor just a little, because I *really* like *this* one: Earth is the *third* planet in a system which features only one life sustaining planet, consisting of *three* times *three*, planets in all, (nine).

However, defining the nature of the Trinity (which only rings true to me for the reasons outlined above, not because some religious authority figure told me I should, which is never a good reason to accept *anything* as absolute truth because besides being a barrier to ones own ability to think things through, about the nature of life, God, and man, it also can be the root of fundamentalism, which leads to fanaticism) is not what's most important to me as I try to come to terms with my own thoughts and feelings regarding the human experience. I'll leave the mystical hair-splitting to theologians. And besides, throughout the history of Christianity these debates have led more to divisiveness than anything else.

What I think *does* matter most doesn't lead me to aspire to being a Christian evangelist, so I'm not writing this to preach, but to "flesh" out (as it were), what my personal answer to the God question is. I outright reject any assertions which posit that non-believers aren't "saved," and therefore, spiritually doomed. Such notions are patent nonsense. I have little patience for exclusivity and fundamentalism in Christianity (or anywhere for that matter), as they are positively antithetical to what my deepest sense of what Jesus Is. If it *is* indeed true that the absolute source of all existence in any form personified among *us*, well than it *is* just that, and will remain so whether all people everywhere recognize it or not. Yes, it would indeed be true for each and every human being who has ever lived whether they have ever heard about it or not, or whether they have heard it and didn't believe it. For instance, I'm absolutely convinced that atheists are going to be some of the most surprised and delighted people in Heaven! Can you just imagine the average family-loving, law abiding atheist scientist, after having lived a life of learning, contributing and caring for others, arriving in whatever Heaven is and exclaiming "No way! There *is* an afterlife after all!" And what's that you say? Christ personified for *me* as much as anybody else? What an awesome God!

Chapter 14
He Believes in *You*

There was a life-changing line in a relatively recent remake of the movie *The Count Of Monte Christo*, where Richard Harris, an old, learned man of faith, is dying in his prison cell with his cellmate played by Jim Caveziel, an innocent man beaten and tortured regularly and who has come to reject the idea of God, and who had become Harris' student. The Harris character mentions God, while dying, in his final words to Caveziel's character who in turn defiantly rebukes him saying "but I don't believe in God," and with his final breath, Harris (who in true life, wasn't long for this world) peacefully says to him, with the most beautiful, knowing resolve, "It doesn't matter, He believes in *you*." This simple phrase strikes the most profound chord deep within me, emotionally and spiritually, about the kind of God that created everything and everyone. For what kind of God indeed would create humans who are spread all over an entire planet and punish whole peoples in remote corners of that planet, far from the large cities and populated areas, that didn't hear about God participating in humanity (this of course being a matter of faith) and "damn" them for it? This kind of thinking and proselytizing has, in my view, given Christianity a bad name over the centuries from the point of view of other religions and of atheists.

Christians who believe that non-Christians will in some way be disenfranchised from God, believe in a God that is, to me, wholly irreconcilable to the universally loving and forgiving God demonstrated by Jesus. But people can be unreasonable. *That* unfortunately, I can comprehend. However, I *cannot* comprehend the idea of *God* being unreasonable. Especially if that God became a human, participated in all the different ups and downs that flesh is heir to, a God who would've known that people in organized government and/or religion (no matter *where* in the world this would've taken place) would persecute, prosecute and execute any individual claiming to be the Son of, or one and the same with, God. This God would've been aware of human nature, aware of fear and loathing, and aware of its lethal consequences. Therefore, a God that would participate in humanity *despite* knowing this, would be a God of infinite patience and unconditional love and forgiveness. This doesn't sound like an unreasonable, "exclusive-club" God to me.

He would've known too, of the grizzly form of execution popular at the time and place chosen for the incarnation. But that didn't stop him from joining us. He—(by the way, I use the word "He," hoping the gender sensitive will forgive me, in reference to God, not so much as a function of classic, patriarchal thinking, as wanting to avoiding using He/She/It every time I refer to God. I don't really perceive God as a thing so "It" goes, and I really don't perceive God as having either gender because God *must* be pure Spirit, so I'm only using "He" because it's easy. Okay, alright, alright, maybe I *am* a *little* gender conditioned!) (Truthfully, my first mental image of God, when I was a little boy, was of a woman with red hair down to her feet; only God knows I'm being honest about that!) Anyway, He would've known too, that many would, at that time and in later times, not believe him to be God. Holding this against them would be a *human* reaction, not a reaction of a God willing to submit to what He submitted to.

I fully realize that there are quotes in the Gospels referring to non-believers not being welcomed into God's presence, because at least one of them cite Jesus as saying "no one comes to the Father, except through me." (John 14:6) My first point in this regard would be that the four Gospel texts are inconsistent with each other and this alone speaks to both human error and translation issues, not to mention interpretation issues as well. For even if He *did* say this, or something similar, it *could* be the case that, the true sense of what was said could either be lost in translation or misinterpreted and can be something that was meant to communicate the idea that in the afterlife, when coming into God's presence, one would then come to realize absolute truth (because if it *is* truth, Jesus being God that is, than in the most absolute sense it wouldn't be deniable when one's spirit comes into the presence of God in the afterlife) and recognize the true face of God. Who knows? Perhaps, if free will continues as the spirit carries on after death (again this is all faith and conjecture) and one chooses to reject Jesus even when faced with the absolute knowledge that He is truth, than maybe one's spirit would voluntarily exist away from God. This would be my idea of hell, not fire and brimstone and nonsense, but simply not being with God. This existence, in some abstract, cold void, would have to be, in my view, an existence *chosen* by an individual soul/consciousness. This idea would also hearken back to, and be consistent with, the notion of a non-tyrannical God for the simple reason that this theory allows for free will and freedom of choice to be the ultimate, supreme, determining factor in the fate of ones immortal soul, instead of something force fed or programmed into a soul by God.

As for those who indeed commit atrocity during life: I'm sure there is some form of justice or penance or *something*, that only God is capable of fully seeing and understanding, awaiting those who commit heinous atrocities in life, which would balance things out and make things right. Maybe their souls *are* discarded: the Hitler's, Stalin's, torturers, murderers, rapist's and oppressors of history: That, I leave up to God. I have to. If there *is* a God there *will* be some form of final justice; the nature of which, only God knows: If there is not, than no final justice is possible. However, it is positively insane to believe in a God who would impose punishment on people who don't believe in Jesus during their lives on Earth. I'm sorry, but it's just that I've known, do know, and will know, *far* too many selfless, kind hearted, loving, caring, providing and forgiving people who happen to be either non-Christian or atheist and nobody is going to tell *me* that they will be excluded from God's presence when their lives are through: Period. And what wrongs us common folk do during life, again, if there is a God, will be something that God sorts out in his infinite wisdom. I'm personally convinced that if we *are* truly sorry for our wrongs, and ask God for forgiveness, that we will indeed be forgiven.

Forgiveness brings me back to the Jesus question overall. I referred previously to the idea that God would've known, being the creator of human nature and free will, that state and religious authorities would wind up executing, and probably pretty gruesomely, anybody claiming to be God personified. Religion, being a very volatile animal purely by way of the fact that almost every religion believes itself to be privy to exclusive truth and all the explosive emotions which are entwined with such beliefs, fear and loathing being among them, often lead to violence in and of itself. And state authorities being concerned with quelling any social upheavals or revolutions that can be ignited by religious zeal, would inevitably come into play in *any* historical context where a seemingly mortal man claims divinity: Or what if Jesus was living in an atheistic totalitarian regime of some sort, he would've been executed with no religious involvement at all. The point is, God was willing to lovingly close the rift between Himself and people, right and wrong, and life and death by submitting to victimization caused by fear and loathing. The popular phrase often offered in an attempt to explain violence and war that says these are examples of man's inhumanity to man I think is accurate.

Chapter 15
Closing the Rifts

Now, to get back to those three rifts. First: God and people had to be *separated* by sheer virtue of people having to exist at all in order to render existence meritorious, while God continued(s) to exist in omnipresence, omniscience and omnipotence. This one is closed by God personifying in the first place, taking on the fragile frame of humanity. Second, a rift is further created by the necessity of duality and free will: both had to exist for frame of reference, and in order for meaning and merit to belong to things like goodness borne of free will as opposed to violence of free will, light as opposed to dark, apathy as opposed to compassion, and love as opposed to hate. In a free-will based universe, inevitably, there would be those who choose wrongful and homicidal conduct. This would be closed by Jesus forgiving; in particular, those who chose to torture and execute and mock him, and in general those who choose to commit wrongful acts.

Closing the rift between right and wrong by being a victim; pretty radical idea huh? I'm sure though, that there are those who would ask "If Jesus was/is God, why would he allow people to torture him when he, if he *were* God, would have the power to destroy them and their intentions with a mere whim?" He is omnipotent (all-powerful) right? And being so, he can forcibly correct perpetrators of wrong doing by show of punitive might so that they would be afraid to do wrong, let alone try to kill the Christ, the anointed one, the personification of the Almighty, right? Maybe there would've been those present at the crucifixion challenging him to come off of the cross as cited in the Gospels. I think and believe the answer to this is that much of the purpose of Jesus' life and submission to the ill effects of free will gone awry would've been for the sake of the ultimate demonstration of unconditional love and forgiveness, not the ultimate demonstration of might: *The Wounded Healer* (a book by Henri Nouen S.J.). It sounds like a contradiction in terms, but in a Christian universe, it makes sense. It's hard to accept, but it makes sense: The ultimate healing being accomplished by a personified God receiving the same cruel treatment that people throughout the ages have endured by those who chose violence and cruelty, yet *forgiving* them for it. It's the ultimate demonstration of stopping the seemingly endless cycles of revenge. There can never be a permanent, true peace on Earth until there is an end to the cycles of revenge. Jesus demonstrated it. It *can* be done.

The ability to do so doesn't seem to be manifest in the collective human community but the ability *is*, I believe, available to us. I know how profoundly hard it is to stop the cycles of revenge within my own heart so I think I can appreciate how monumentally hard such a thing would be for the human race to do as a whole.

For example, I'll never forget (and please understand, I'm not proud of the emotions I'm about to share but I do so for the sake of honesty and of acknowledgment of how hard, but how important, it would be for humanity to break the cycles), the morning of September 11th 2001, after having witnessed the second plane impact the South Tower and knowing it to be a terrorist attack, a short while later, at the time of the North

Tower's collapse, the fear of the moment gave way to unmitigated rage as I realized what just happened to working New Yorkers filling that building and I could contain myself no longer. Myself and the co-worker driving the telephone company truck I was in pulled over and stopped because the driver had just witnessed something absolutely *unfathomable* in his rear view mirror. He gasped something to the effect of "Oh my God Chris! The World Trade Center just *collapsed!*"

I jumped out of the truck to the sounds of women screaming. Having been told by cops and firemen to leave the downtown area, we began driving north. We were in west Greenwich Village at that moment but people walking south on that clear morning had full view of the unthinkable cataclysm as it occurred before their horrified, disbelieving eyes. Their agony for their fellow human beings was unbearable, and absolutely palpable. It fueled in me, by far, the most venomous, hate filled explosion of rage I have ever experienced in my entire life or even imagined myself capable of feeling. The battle-cry like yell that came out of me was animal-like. I utterly gave in to the most violent surge of hate that I have ever experienced in my time on this planet and I pray to never experience it again. *It is a cancer of the soul.* It decays away that which is good within a person, or certainly can, over time. But within that moment, the thing that made the rage explode like Mt. Saint Helen as opposed to just any lava spewing volcanic eruption, was the *revenge* part: *for the very reason that I knew there could be none!* It had already been stewing in my mind and heart, mixed with fear and sorrow for those in the upper floors, that the perpetrators where the modern day, terrorist equivalent to Kamikaze pilots, and so punishing them was not a satisfaction America would ever enjoy (for lack of a better word). But I wanted to rage out of my skin and strangle their very souls.

I felt these emotions, I believe, because it is human to do so. But I think God showed us that we can, if we want to, eventually transcend such hatred. It would have to be the entire human race collectively desiring an end to the madness, so it would *seem* impossible. But I personally hold out hope for the future. I know how naive that sounds. Especially since I fully acknowledge that retaliation against the Taliban regime (the regime in Afghanistan which aided and abetted the terrorists behind the 9/11 attacks) was a necessary act of national self defense, and we must, in my view, actively pursue the leader of, and any members of, the Al Qaeda terrorist network for the sake of national defense. But for the future of mankind, in order for the human race to fully evolve, the madness has to stop. And I believe that Jesus demonstrated that and closed the second rift.

To help illustrate this, let's go back to our mental imagery workshop. (Not to worry, we'll get to that third rift or third "aspect" of the Great Rift afterwards). Let's imagine, in a hypothetical scenario, that we somehow know for sure that there is indeed a God, and also, by some hypothetical knowledge, we know with certainty, that God became a man. If the above questions (the ones about the almighty allowing harm to be inflicted on him) were answered in the human way, then we would see Jesus bringing the soldiers who came to arrest him to their knees in pain and submission. We would see Jesus not only refraining from telling Peter to stand down when he drew his sword and struck a guard, but allowing full scale war between his followers and those who would arrest him: War that would be a futile, hopeless cause for his enemies, for he was God Almighty, present here on Earth. There would be no nocturnal convening of high priests for the purpose of conducting a hearing of religious elders condemning him for blasphemy. He would have power over their minds and he would have ability to control them and make them behave in any manner he saw fit and to believe in anything he told them to believe. There would be no scourging because soldiers of the state would fall, helpless before him and lifeless in his wake. There would be no crucifixion because the local procurator and his forces would be annihilated when they attempted to carry out their terrible execution. And everyone, everywhere, would be put on permanent notice that to defy God means suicide of body and soul alike.

Now, what would God, or people, I ask you, gain from this arrangement? People for all times would behave well for exactly all the wrong reasons. Fear of punishment is an incomplete reason to refrain from wrongful behavior. And conversely, acts of goodness aren't really acts of goodness or kindness at all if they are only done out of fear of the invisible tyrant that will punish you if you don't perform good deeds, or for attention or gain.

True kindness only has any merit and meaning if it is offered of free will and not motivated by a desire for reward. I realize this is basic Kantian ethics. Emmanuel Kant called his system of ethics "Deontology," a system of moral conduct criteria based on what he called a "categorical imperative," doing something selfless for no reason other than that the doing is right and good, not because the doer or the society would benefit in some way. This code of moral conduct rings true for me, because it is consistent with universal law that is not bound to guilt based, reward and punishment criteria, but the good and the right in the Socratic sense being strove for in the most pure, absolute measure, simply for it's own sake. Acts of charity, compassion, forgiveness and love that are done without motivation, but only pure feeling, are ultimately all apart of the supreme source of goodness which, if there is a God, must reside in all of us as a by-product of being "created." Only such pure, unmitigated and unconditional love can close the rift created by the separation of God and people which is a function of the physical being inherently separate from the non-physical, source of existence; time from the timeless, temporal from the eternal. This brings me back to the idea of a personified God closing the third rift in the God/People equation.

Chapter 16
The Third Rift

Now, the third and possibly most prominent rift between creator and created is mortality vs. immortality, of course. Anything existing in the physical universe cannot endure for time that stretches out to endless infinity, not even stars; they too are subject to the laws of the temporal, which include inevitable change and demise. Some forms of life right here on earth live for hundreds of years (California Redwoods), but must ultimately give way to the cycles of life and death. In a Godless scenario, death may be a part of life but is not the portal to the next form of existence (whatever that may be) which many believe it to be. However, even in a *created* universe, death in general and our own mortality in particular are often so hard to come to terms with that we simply put it out of our minds rather than contemplate it, let alone embrace it. For time out of mind, people from different cultures all over the world have longed for immortality, either by finding a literal "fountain of youth" or by figurative ways such as one's progeny or one's lifeworks. We can't—and understandably so, I think—accept the idea of being a cosmic flash-in-the-pan: popping into an accidental existence by pure chance and returning to the void from which we came without at least leaving our mark. Why is it so important to us to make it known that we were here? There are images carved into cave walls from the earliest man because even pre-civilized man (people) didn't want to be the tree that fell in the forest without making a sound. We seem to have it hard wired in our very DNA that life is fleeting so we desperately need affirmation that we do indeed matter, that our stay here on Earth had meaning: Meaning that isn't limited to ourselves either, but that plays a role in a much broader picture.

This all resonates with me to the tune of a God-based universe. As life forms, even Amoeba and Protozoa are born, metabolize and die, but *we* are, as Judy Collins once put it: *"stardust, we are golden, we are million-year-old carbon, and we got to get ourselves back to the garden."* We seem to have an innate awareness; that we are special and have a source from which we emanated and to which we will return. Yet most confounding of all is the seeming fact that there is no way to know this with certainty. We find losing loved one's unbearable and most of us can't contemplate our own demise without at least some degree of anxiety, if not outright terror. Death has been called the ultimate mystery and I think rightly so. What kind of God would force us to deal (or not deal, as the case may be) with such an uncertain reality? Only a tyrant would throw us to the wolves of uncertainty, pain and mortality if there were no great incomprehensible love behind it. What kind of God would, with his silence, effectively tell us "You're on your own, I'm immortal since time immemorial and will be for all eternity. Your reality of death and the physical, mental and spiritual anguish it causes is *your* problem, not mine. I'm God!" A pretty cold One would say such things I think. A cold and indifferent God?: A source of all existence that is basically a cosmic curmudgeon? It just doesn't make sense. It is reconcilable to neither reason nor intuition. It just doesn't feel right.

So what then *does* reconcile to reason *and* "feel" right? What do I find myself returning to again and again when I calm down after fits of fury and rage directed toward the night sky as I lay awake in bed? What represents the hope of a God who is neither indifferent nor cold and curmudgeonly and which understands our anger, sorrow and desperation concerning the anguish of the human condition? What can encapsulate the idea of a kind of God that is not only transcendent of, but which is *empathic* towards, our desperately inconsolable, incomprehensible, un-namable, sublime sorrow over this greatest of all mysteries and how it seemingly separates us forever from the ones we love? I think the answer is One which would be, not because of being a God that *has* to, but One which is *willing* to, close the rift between life and death and God and man by *participating* in all aspects of the human condition. These, of course would necessarily include birth and the dependency of infancy, childhood and all it's woes, and adult life and all the anguish that *it* can bring, including doubt, sorrow, effort, learning, and grieving, which are all part and parcel of the human experience. Also, he would have to be One which is willing to pass through death; a physically excruciating death. And would be willing to do so as *Thee Perfect Act of Love And Reconciliation.* Not *because* of the sins of man, but *despite them!* This is about *Love* not *guilt*! This is *not* about God, in effect, telling us: ...Now see what you've done Humankind? Now I have to go through agony and death for you! Thus putting the blame for Jesus' passion and death on us all: All of us who have ever lived; when what rings true judging from Jesus' words and deeds is, it wasn't a reconciliation that *had* to be, but one that God *chose* and that Jesus *willingly accepted.*

This is pure Love we're talking about here, unconditional, unmitigated, pure Love. And it closes the rift between life &

death, God & man, and the temporal & eternal, by way of his bodily resurrection (which again, of course, is purely a matter of faith) because we are shown that death is not the end, but only a transition. And Jesus is the connecting bridge between death and life. Therefore, death, in effect, has been defeated and has been shown to us by God not to be final for the inner life that animates us all: Indeed, that life goes on.

Chapter 17
Setting the Record Straight

Now, the idea of The Passion (the beating, scourging and crucifixion of Jesus), being a blame game ridden with guilt and fear of punishment is a profoundly damaging one. It is a distortion and a misrepresentation of what Christianity essentially is: Love and Forgiveness. And it gives Christianity a *bad* name. It leads to some of the most misguided terms I've ever heard in the English language when it comes to Christianity. Terms like "Christ Killer." The record has to be set straight once and for all with this nonsense.

I once worked as a clerk at the Montefiore Medical Center in the Bronx and my manager was one of the nicest, most affable and gracious people I have ever had the pleasure of working for. Her name was Eve (of all things). Eve treated us clerks more like a motherly school teacher would than a boss. She was kind and considerate. I mention all of this because of how sad, shameful and infuriating it is that this lovely person of such good temperament and disposition went through a childhood in England as a young Jewish girl being bullied and taunted by other children who clearly had been exposed to anti-Semitic influence in their environments.

Eve told me a story of being a very young little girl going about her business of a school day and being stopped, bullied, harassed and harangued by other children who were being raised as Christians. She would be accosted by a group of children who would push her against a wall and jab at her chest with accusatory fingers insisting "you killed our Lord!" This would invariably be accompanied by whatever anti-Semitic slurs the kids had learned. She would be hurt and confused and go home crying. What had *she* done to *anybody's* Lord? she would wonder. As they had occurred during her formative years, Eve grew up with these experiences indelibly imprinted on her consciousness as her impression of what Christians believe and how they interact with people of other faiths, in short, what Christianity *is* from her experience.

I was embarrassed and angered by her story. This was not a faith of love, compassion and forgiveness being taught to these children. Yet I was still rather historically uninformed and more than a little naive. I had yet to learn the gruesome details of the Crusades. I had yet to learn of the centuries of Catholic and Protestant anti-Semitism throughout Europe. I had yet to learn of the failure of Pope Pius XII to condemn the holocaust of six million Jewish people after World War II. I had yet to learn that so very many people use the term "Christ Killer" referring to Jewish people. And to my intense chagrin, I began realizing that my faith, a faith based on the purest and most unconditional love, had long since been twisted, distorted and completely misrepresented, largely by it's chief purveyors, into one of guilt, shame and blame concerning the death of Jesus of Nazareth.

Should I fail to make anything else clear in this book let the following be set down once and for all The Ages: The reason Christ personified (of course, the word "Christ" is not a name, but a title, linguistically originating from the Greek, meaning "anointed one") was to "testify to the Truth" (John 18:37). Part and parcel of that living testimony was the inevitable execution and resurrection of the body animated by Christ. *If anything was ever pre-ordained (and I've already discussed my conviction that it would be senseless for God to pre-program each individuals' destiny a priori, which would trash free will from eternity, it was this: That no matter where and when this personification were to take place, it would culminate in violent death and a faith would begin with a resurrection).*

In plain English: Jesus *had* to suffer and die. And most important, He did so willingly and with perfect love and forgiveness to mend the aforementioned rifts between Creator and created. He did so willingly, I say again, not *because* of our willful wrongs but *despite them!* This was about *love* not *guilt!* Why God chose to personify in any given time and place can only be guessed at. It conceivably could be that the Jewish people were historically the first to openly declare a monotheistic religion (a belief in a single, omnipotent, omnipresent, omniscient God) but that's just a guess, who knows? Who *can* know? This is all a matter of faith. But I don't invest my faith and heart in anything I can't reconcile to reason, before making the leap. And reason tells me that no matter where and when on Earth this personification would've taken place, knowing human nature, knowing that the secular and religious always clash, a person being followed by large crowds who eventually openly declares himself to be the Son of God, before religious and state authorities alike, would cause fear and loathing. Our ugly friends fear and loathing, as we all know, always lead to violence, and in the case of one whose claims threaten either the political powers that be, or the religious; death. For those who would pooh this and say "oh, in modern times such a person would be regarded as insane or kooky and institutionalized"; I give you Mahatma Gandhi and Martin Luther King Jr., neither of whom claimed to be God!

Therefore, if you've been raised by any Christian tradition which has imbedded in you a sense that there are individuals or whole peoples to *blame* for Jesus' death, you have been taught *wrongly.* Furthermore, if you have been taught that anyone who doesn't believe in Jesus is doomed to damnation, you have been taught *wrongly.* For goodness sake, what kind of Cosmic Tyrant would dispose of souls into some inter-dimensional trash dumpster just because they were born at a time and place which made them unaware of Jesus' participation in humanity, and his death and resurrection?

Or, what kind of unreasonable Omnipotent Bully would discard the souls of the many millions throughout history born into the other faiths and traditions of the world? If you believe Jesus instructed the faithful to go out into the world and spread the good news, do so with *how* you live, not by attempting to convert people of other traditions. Let Christians be recognized by their *love,* not their *zeal.* Christianity has earned the reputation of being intolerant and judgmental: nothing could be more antithetical to the faith. These things have lead to the forceful conversion of people all over the world. I can just imagine Jesus smacking his palm to his forehead and exasperatingly saying through a sigh, *"this isn't what I had in mind, kids."* So, whenever, *anybody* tells you that they and their cronies have exclusive privy and domain over *absolute* truth: *RUN!* There is no communicating reasonably with such people.

Chapter 18
Passion Over *The Passion*

Recently, a Hollywood movie which depicts the final hours in the life of Jesus of Nazareth caused quite a controversy: Mostly because it was accused of promoting anti-Semitism, and also because of its brutal, graphic realism during the scourging sequence.

I myself am a huge fan of the maker of this movie, Mel Gibson. For me, he demonstrated the depth of his talent and separated himself from the action hero typecast he was falling into when he portrayed Hamlet in the 1990 movie production by Franco Zeffirelli A few years later, the full breadth and scope of this movie visionary was revealed in what could be one of the greatest period epics ever filmed, *Braveheart*, which Gibson wrote, directed and starred in.

So I brought much admiration for Gibson's work with me when I thought I would find out what all the hoopla is all about and see his latest film: *The Passion of The Christ*. (I choose to discuss it here because it is relevant to my previous section concerning anti-Semitic behavior in Christian history.) There was much concern in the Jewish community that anti-Semitic furor might lead to hostility or even violence as a result of the movie because, historically, especially in early 20th century German Passion Plays, and indeed, throughout Europe, such hostility *did* result from the performances of the drama. It again brings up the blame and guilt issue over Jesus' execution, wittingly or not on Gibson's part.

What was most disturbing to me about the controversy over this film was not whether it was indeed guilty of "blaming" the Jews for Jesus' death, but that such ramped and pervasive lack of insight in this regard still prevails in this day and age. For this, I largely blame the Catholic Church, especially since it wasn't until 1965, during the Second Vatican Council, under Pope John the 26th, that the Church officially announced an apology for blaming the Jews for Jesus' crucifixion. You would think the Church whose first Pope was a close friend of Jesus himself, Simon Peter, would've, many centuries ago, had the insight and clarity of understanding that most of Jesus' mission on Earth was intrinsically entwined with his inevitable execution, allowing for the cornerstone of the Christian tradition, His resurrection. And that blame and guilt had nothing to do with it, that it would've come to pass this way irrespective of the time and location of Jesus' earthly ministry.

So, getting back to *The Passion*: Did I myself, in an attempt at being purely objective and not wanting to feel defensive for Gibson's sake, find the film to incite anti-Semitism? No. I did not find anti-Semitism in its depiction of the Sanhedrin and other Jewish authorities. However, I did find one thing disturbing in its *subtle* inclusion of a line spoken but not included in the English subtitles. (The movie's dialogue was spoken in Aramaic and Latin). At one point, when debating what Jesus' fate must legally be according to the Jewish Laws of the time, the Aramaic equivalent to "his blood will be on our hands and the hands of our descendants" was uttered in the audio background. Gibson was accused of doing so deliberately to cause an anti-Semitic reaction. Now, can I be certain in my heart that Mel Gibson doesn't harbor any negative emotions toward Jews? No. Does it matter whether he does?

NO! If so, he would be just another so-called Christian who simply doesn't get it. Anybody who blames the Jews or Romans or anybody else and thinks Jesus was supposed to have lived until a ripe old age, settling down in the suburbs of Jerusalem, raising a family and collecting his carpentry pension while taking power walks on water and fishing on Sundays, just *doesn't get it!*

As to the details: Look, there were two realities present at a time and place in history where religious fanaticism was prevalent and being tolerated by a large, powerful Empire with local procurators charged with governing the various jurisdictions too far removed from the center of power to be dealt with directly by the Emperor. Of course I'm speaking of the Roman Empire approximately 2000 years ago under Caesar Tiberius. The province of Judea, including present day Israel, then Palestine, is where Jesus brought attention to himself by the religious and state authorities which culminated in his execution. According to the Gospels, our primary source for both Jesus' historic and debated activities alike, Jesus lost his temper at the great Jewish Temple in Jerusalem over money changing activities, overturning tables and nearly, if not outright, causing a riot. We understand he shouted something to the effect of destroying and rebuilding the Temple in three days in the heat of his fury. For believers, he was clearly making one of his metaphoric references, this time to his death and resurrection after three days, his body being the symbolic temple. However, in the actual moment at that time and place, it was taken to be meant literally and was therefore regarded as a threat to the religious establishment. And it also had been getting around that he had referred to himself as the Son of God, a claim punishable by death according to the Jewish religious laws of the day. Now whether it is truly right and proper to execute someone for claiming to be God is immaterial here, as discussed above. It simply was the reality of the time and place in history.

As for the Roman picture, the local Governor or "Procurator" was charged by the Emperor with keeping the peace and maintaining order in his province. A man by the name of Pontius Pilate was the Procurator of Judea. What we know for certain about the character of the man is limited. The Gospels portray him as a man who saw no executable offense in the words or deeds of Jesus, but one who condescended to the apparent blood thirst of a crowd gathered at his court which had chosen by show of cheers and jeers to release a criminal Zealot by the name of Barabbas when offered a choice in a show of Passover clemency to release either Jesus or Barabbas. Pilate chose to "wash his hands" of Jesus' blood and ordered his crucifixion.

Does this make Pilate "blamable" for the death of Jesus? Quite simply: No. Our impression of Pilate, besides the Gospels, largely comes from classic movies that depict him as an indifferent, exasperated, pragmatic purveyor of Roman justice. We are given the impression he was kind of a good guy who caved in to pressure and who even pleaded with Jesus to speak up and defend himself. But what was the true nature of his character? We just can't know, and frankly, it doesn't matter. Historians take exception with the frustrated seeker of fair play persona generated by the Gospels and movies. They mostly agree that Pontius Pilate was ruthless and brutal in the execution of his office. Which one is true and correct? It doesn't matter.

It was the combination of circumstance and collective, cumulative human nature which would have lead to this inevitable climax to Jesus' ministry on Earth. The fact that it also represented a new beginning as the necessary gateway to the resurrection is, of course, a matter of faith. But, as outlined in previous sections, it closed the rift between God and people and represented the ONE all important divine intervention and interaction between God and humankind: *The Ultimate Singularity*. It is the single, all important answer to the question of why God doesn't intervene in human affairs. To do so would be to meddle with the very purpose of His own creation, the affirmation of free will, compassion and love. And this despite the horrors of human suffering and death, caused by both nature and man.

What kind of God would *not* participate in the suffering of humankind and reconcile with all people for all time with this single all important intervention in the form of personification, living, loving, suffering, teaching, dying and rising? I don't know what kind, but it's not a kind that resonates with my personal years of living, thinking and feeling about the human condition and human experience in relation to a God that often *seems* to be an absentee cosmic landlord, but One who is actually, infinitely, lovingly, quite resident.

So please, let's leave the blame game out of the Jesus question once and for all. It's simply horribly inconsistent with a thoroughly thought through analysis of the faith.

And yes, this includes Judas Iscariot. I feel this also bears clarification as to the nature of God and the "what kind" question. In classic artists' rendering of Jesus in Heaven with his Apostles, Judas is conspicuously absent, suggesting of course, that he didn't make the trip. This I cannot reconcile to a reasonable God. It is actually believed by many that Judas was condemned to hell for his betrayal of Jesus. Jesus came into this world to die and rise. Now I ask you once again, what kind of unreasonable nut job of absolute cosmic tyranny would eternally damn one who was actually just a cog in the wheel of circumstance? We should remember that Judas just had the wrong idea about what Jesus' mission should be. Iscariot's zeal blinded him to the larger picture, which few, if any, could perceive in real time. Judas probably thought that Jesus should lead a military revolt against the Roman Empire. Something that was indeed to take place just 80 some odd years after, and as we know, end tragically high atop Masada.

To know exactly what would've been on Judas' mind as far as why he would've disclosed Jesus' whereabouts to the Sanhedrin can only be guessed at. I prefer the theory proposed in Franco Zeffirelli's 1977 television production *Jesus of Nazareth*.

In this film Iscariot is portrayed as being convinced that if the Jewish High Priests and Elders were to hear Jesus make his case in person, that he would be embraced, as a teacher and leader: To exactly what end, isn't postulated, but he is not demonized in this movie, and I think rightly so. (Mortals have no business deciding whose eternal soul should be disposed of. This is why the whole idea of excommunication is so offensive to my sensibilities of what a fair and just God is. I won't believe in a God that stands by and allows short sighted, judgmental hypocrites to mete out eternal justice here on Earth).

Therefore, in Jesus of Nazereth I think Zeffirelli's approach was right on. It showed Judas in agony over having been indirectly the cause of Jesus' trial and crucifixion, and hanging himself in shame and remorse. I think it best to let God be the one to decide the fate of such a one don't you? I think if we have faith in the existence of God, particularly such a loving One, we would be best advised to let *God* handle the God stuff. For my part, if Judas went through emotional hell enough to take his own life, and asked God for forgiveness, I'll let God do the God stuff, but I believe he would've been forgiven by a Perfect and Just, Loving God.

Chapter 19
The Resurrection:
The Great Quantum Leap of Faith

The sun (son?) rises in the east, and so we get the word "Easter." What a perfectly beautiful and clever metaphor and play on words. But did the Son of God (God incarnate, The Christ made human) literally come back to bodily life after having lain dead for three days? Obviously, few things could more defy science and biological reality. After all, dead is dead. Most objective minds, I'm sure, would simply say that anybody seen walking around three days after having been crucified might have been badly injured but was never dead in the first place: An understandable presumption. But the very fact that "dead is dead" is seen as the ultimate finality to human existence, I submit, is a very large part of why Christ went through death in the first place: To demonstrate (aside from another, huge piece of why Jesus died: To not ask us to go through *anything* he would not be willing to go through himself, with and for us) personally that, no; such absolute finality is indeed *not* the case. As I've covered previously, there is no discernable, clear divine intervention in human affairs throughout history. Therefore, as far as God directly interacting with people on Earth is concerned, this is the biggie, the Be All End All. The "Once And For All Time" intervention between God and humankind.

But wait a minute: What kind of God would go through all of this and leave us nothing but an oral tradition of it ever having happened and then, a generation or so later, let the writing take on four inconsistent accounts? Shouldn't He have marched right into Pilate's court, smiling, resplendent in white and healthy of pallor, announcing his glorious resurrection? Shouldn't He have strolled right into the High Priests presence in the Temple, letting Ciaphas see the wounds that clearly should've left him permanently dead, hugging him and saying, "Don't worry, it's all good!" Indeed, why didn't he bi-locate these appearances simultaneously, proving his reality further? As a matter of fact why didn't He multiple-locate all over the world, announcing that God and People are reconciled for all time, and that life goes on eternally, not to worry, we are all spiritual beings going through a human experience and we will all reunite with lost loved ones in timeless eternity with God? It's a good question right? Why insist it be a matter of faith? My offering would be that God knows human nature pretty darn well. And in so knowing, would've been fully aware that Pilate and the Roman authorities in general would only have claimed that some magic trick had been perpetrated, some hocus-pocus and sorcery must have been at play here, that this is no God, but a hoax being pulled off by yet another "wanna-be" messianic figure at a time when the streets of Judea were replete with prophets, charlatans and Jewish messiahs.

Reaction from religious authorities would've been scarcely different. Temple officials would likely have claimed that He simply was never dead to begin with, and that this blasphemer must be silenced once and for all. You then might ask: Well, why didn't he let them try? If this was the One and only Omnipotent God, why didn't he simply tell them "do your worst"? He could've shown himself impervious to harm and in so doing *make* them accept that He is Absolute Reality itself, Life that cannot be extinguished. Why?: because that would be a matter of *forcing* people to accept something that was done out of Love, not *will to power*. This was not about scaring people into belief or submission. Jesus having gone through that agonizing death was about perfect Humility, Grace, Forgiveness and Love: Therein lies the nature of the perfect God, not exercising power, forcibly imposed, but unconditional Love, fully aware that even having gone through it all, that this perfect act of love would be rejected after the fact, by many. Therefore, it's not that God insists that belief in the resurrection be a matter of faith because He is vain and egotistical, but that it simply can *be* no other way. *If it is indeed absolute reality, then no absence of belief can ever make it not so, and no proof need ever be displayed: it simply is.*

God knows that life is rife with hardship of all kinds, so he participated in humanity out of Love, and I can't see a reasonable God wanting to be feared: If God *wants* or *desires* (human concepts by the way) *anything*, it must be our free-will-based love. I think an infinite, perfect, unconditionally loving God would love us even when we don't love back, but I have to think that if anything warms His infinite spirit, it's feeling us loving each other and Him, not because we're told or commanded to, but because we simply, genuinely, freely and truly *do*.

It's the next and final phase in human evolution, folks: Love for Love's sake out of purely free will despite the hardships of human existence. As corny as it sounds in an early twenty-first century world filled with hate, intolerance and war, songsmith Burt Bacharach had it right in his classic song "W*hat the world needs now, is Love, sweet Love, it's the only thing that there's just too little of.*"

Chapter 20
The Realities of Everyday Life (and Death) on Earth

I can hear it now, because the like has been heard so many times: "oh don't give me that sappy love crap, it doesn't pay my bills or prevent earthquakes, tsunamis, hurricanes, cyclones, or disease!" And how right you would be, in your reality check of the harshness of life on Earth: After all, free will is one thing, but what kind of God allows natural catastrophes like the tsunami of Southeast Asia in 2004? Many Christians couldn't help but observe a certain irony in the fact that the tsunami struck so many hundreds of thousands of innocents the very day after Christmas. Where was your "God" or your "Jesus" when rushing tidal waves ripped children from their mothers' arms, swept away mercilessly by indifferent nature?

Indeed, why are things the way they are in nature if God so loves, or indeed, if there is a God at all? Doesn't it seem coolly indifferent at best, or at worst, cold hearted and tyrannical to create people and leave them stranded amid the harshness of nature and subject to the endless myriad of pain and suffering that is part of the human experience? Obviously it's as old a question as any in human inquiry and is also a very tough one to tackle, and so must be wrestled with carefully by the inquisitive mind.

It goes to the very heart and essence of science and theology alike: What is the nature of the matrix of the universe (its mechanical workings) and how did it start? Why is it "set up the way it is"? Science is concerned to render the "what" and theology the "why" for the way the universe works, but both lines of inquiry have intrinsic value. I personally highly value science as a tool for the furtherance of knowledge based on scientific data and empirical evidence, but it can only take us so far when seeking to reach the heart of the matter where the mystery of the human journey is concerned. It tells us with objective clarity and near certainty that all matter in the universe, as observed in the form of galaxies of stars and clusters of galaxies across the nearly inconceivable vastness of the cosmos, is all racing away in all directions, outwardly expanding at dazzling speeds like the dots on a balloon when it is being filled with air.. Physicists tell us that this expansion speaks, empirically, to a common starting point for all matter in the universe. According to this theory, at a single instant the universe burst into existence from a starting point no bigger than a single molecule with an unimaginable explosion of matter and energy that hasn't stopped bursting ever since, of course I'm referring to the "Big Bang."

Over great super-epochs of time that are very hard to appreciate because (aside from the other issues concerning time, the relativity of its nature and it being entwined with both space and individual experience and perception to name a few) we measure time according to physical phenomenon peculiar to our own solar system, which didn't always exist as we know it (in other words, the idea of a "year" only has meaning to us if we have *our* planet revolving around *our* star). Until cosmic gases and other matter slowly cooled and formed our cosmic neighborhood.

But what set this incomprehensible burst of matter and energy into being? Science can retrace the steps using the tools of physics like cosmic forensic investigators to some first billionth of the first "second," but no further. Many believe that the instant of creation wasn't a matter of "creation" at all but a spontaneous phenomenon of cosmic chance, a meaningless accident whereby all the elements and ingredients just happened to congeal at the same "instant." This is an unacceptably unsatisfying answer. And it is where theology and science part company.

For those of us who look at and listen to the results of the Big Bang, including human beings (with their infinite complexities including capacity for a mysterious and ineffable phenomenon we call love, also human intelligence, and creativity), animals, rainbows, sunsets, chocolate, strawberries, stars and newborn babies, it is simply irreconcilable to *reason*, not even faith, to accept the notion that all existence spontaneously erupted out of absolute nothingness and developed its own laws of physics with nothing behind it but the willy-nilly turn of a friendly card! Therefore, and with nothing but the highest regard and immense respect for the scientific method, frankly, it really is a "no-brainer." The question is not whether there *is* a *prima causa*, operating behind it all, but rather, what is the great ultimate reasoning process behind it all?

Couldn't God have simply snapped his fingers and instantaneously popped all of existence, including a finished Earth and Earth's solar system, into being in a willful cosmic blink of an omnipotent eye? I would think so. When you're all powerful you "got it like that" as they say. Apparently, however, He did *not* so choose; according to the indisputable evidence science has shown. And this, it seems, gives us our first clue as to the personality of God and the nature of the great experiment called existence. The merit that free will lends to the human experience piece as discussed earlier also applies (necessarily in conjunction with) to things having to be the way they are concerning the laws, behavior and temperament of nature, on the macro, as well as the micro scale. It seems that God built the programs for the laws of physics into the matrix of the workings of the universe, but chose to "let it be" after that. This would be "Deism" were it not for the all important Jesus piece discussed previously. Why, in His infinite wisdom, did He so chose? We can only speculate, but we can do so with the thoroughly analytic faculties of mind that He also chose to build into *us* in order to reflect back at Him His meritorious, meaningful creation.

In a word: *Authenticity.* It seems clear that a "just add water," instant oatmeal like, instant universe, would sorely and profoundly lack authenticity. It wouldn't have any real merit, and therefore meaning, of its own. Evolution over great eons gives the universe the equivalent of cosmic "street-cred" (a credibility of character based on showing oneself to be the "real thing," not a fabrication or an eminence front of any kind). The universe and its inhabitants have suffered massive growing pains, and it seems that this is the way it simply must be. Does this mean that God is indifferent to our plight as we daily try to cope with the products of the matrix of nature? Gravity from our moon draws moisture up into our atmosphere where it accumulates into clouds which release the rain which is so necessary to life on Earth, but sometimes it rains with terrible fury, and is accompanied by awesome winds, also generated by the laws of physics set into motion and allowed to "be" of natural course, which cause not only flooding and destruction but great human suffering and loss of life. And we must assume that God knew that such would be the case in the grand unfolding of creation from "before" ("before" implies a linear progression in time as in "before-during-and-after," which wouldn't have applied to God operating in a timeless dimension we refer to as "eternity," but I use it to make the point, semantics irrespective) it all began. And I think it stems from a love and belief in us, the created, that transcends simple ideas like "indifference," because even when we don't, won't or can't believe in God, He believes in *us*. I am convinced that the supreme source of existence, of intelligence, of creativity and of love, would give us the benefit of the doubt (despite the fact that we so often fail to reciprocate that benefit) that we can endure the hardships of existence in order to learn, to grow and to spiritually evolve.

What purpose to existence, I dare say (and I realize this takes audacity) what purpose would God himself have if He didn't create souls and a life medium for them to exist *and grow and love through free will* in, if he were to do so with an "instant *perfect* oatmeal" recipe? Therefore, nature must be left to its own devices (and by the way, nature *is* perfect in its way, even though it's often hard on us, but it operates by universal physical laws with consistency and constancy. Action is *always* followed by equal and opposite *reaction*, not only when nature feels like it, and such *has* to be the case, whether or not it's always pleasant, which of course, it often isn't) and the greater cosmic by-product of that sometimes hard fact is *our* growth, *our* evolution and here comes that absolutely all important word again: our *authenticity.*

Let's return to the mental lab of thought experimentation once again to see if we can't flesh this out a bit. Let's imagine a "perfect world." Everyone wants to live in a "perfect world" right? So, what if God went ahead and chose the "instant perfect oatmeal" recipe for existence and simply plopped into existence a universe of purely and utterly undisturbed peace and tranquility; into which would instantaneously pop into existence a planet which wouldn't be the living organism we now know our own planet to truly be, because that would entail planetary metabolism and change which all true life is defined by, but a planet that never belches (when gases in the Earth's interior build up pressure and cause tectonic plates to move, and we all know what happens then) or upon which gravity (one of our universal constants, whatever its *true* nature and definition, whenever you drop something, it falls, and what goes up, must come down, at least within the Earth's atmosphere) doesn't apply consistently because it wouldn't ever rain in a perfect world right? And it wouldn't need to because food and flowers would just grow magically and spontaneously right? Nobody would ever stub their toe while walking through a meadow or stream because there would be no physical laws to allow for it. If someone was looking up at the perfectly cloudless sky and wandered off of a cliff, they would magically float because there would be no danger in a perfect world. Action and re-action would be limited to convenience and never result in hardship. Nobody would have to work at tilling the fields because they would constantly produce crops automatically. Nobody would go hungry. Sounds good right? Sure, sounds great. Wait, it gets better. Nobody would ever get sick, not so much as the sniffles. There would be no bacteria in a perfect world because life wouldn't have been left to evolve naturally; instead it would be forged in a contrived, fabricated way. So: disease? Forget it; no disease would exist in a perfect world. So, nobody would ever have to help their fellow human being get well or get their work done, there would be no need. Nobody would ever have to help or be of service to a fellow human being in need or suffering illness, so no need for compassion would ever arise. Indeed the very concept of compassion would *never come into existence*. There would be no need for it, right? After all, com-passion literally translates to "suffering-with," who needs it, right? Why "suffer" with or *for* anybody? Life is perfect in our perfect world.

So what would people tend to be like in this perfect world? Everyone would be a genius at art and science without ever having to work at it. Nobody would have any musical talent that everyone else doesn't possess equally so why would anybody appreciate anybody else's talents or skills? There would be no social diversity because everybody would be the same. Well wouldn't they? In a "perfect world" nobody would ever have a disagreement regarding *anything—ever.* Everyone would agree on *everything all the time, no exceptions.* Human life, having been instantly contrived, would have no ethnic diversity, because evolution wouldn't have been allowed. So *everyone* on Earth would basically look the same and think the same about everything, always. And cultural diversity?: Forget it. All music and art in which *everyone* shares exactly the same super genius level of talent, would be the same—everywhere. No xenophobia would ever exist because nobody would have to learn to live in the same world as another which is different. Sounds dandy right? And let's not forget the big biggie of them all: there would be no death right? Death is a source of hurt and grief and anxiety and wouldn't exist in our perfect world. Yes, it may well be the gateway to eternal bliss in the presence of God but losing a loved one still causes great heartache right? Nope: there would be none in our perfect world. Everyone would be immortal I guess. So, if I may, I'd like to sum up my sense and feeling for our imaginary perfect world in a single, six letter word: *Boring!* And besides being boring beyond belief, what learning would take place as a result of human life? You know, I find great consolation in the fact that the human condition renders us as incapable of "perfection," that we are inherently flawed in that we can never be omniscient: But what that conversely says is that we can learn, grow and evolve, *indefinitely.* We may not be able to attain perfection but we can *always* improve and expand our knowledge. It removes limitation to our potential! And I must say, I bet God prefers of us to aspire to always push the envelope of human capability in all areas of creativity, science and spiritual and psychological growth and development. What growth of the spirit? What development of character? What transcending of one's own troubles in order to be a part of the bigger picture and experience of compassion would there be, and therefore evolution of the soul, would there be?: None. How could there? I therefore, humbly submit to you, my deeply, deeply appreciated reader; that *things are as they must be.* I love quoting songs, so please indulge me once again: "W*hen I find myself in times of trouble, Mother Mary comes to me, speaking words of wisdom...Let It be." (Paul McCartney).*

Chapter 21
Does God *Want* Us to Suffer, or Could It Be That He *Entrusts* It to Us?

So, if God has blessed me with the grace of insight to make myself clear; suffering must be a part of our journey through life. It's one of those journeys where the essence is in the traveling more than the destination. As I write this, Pope John Paul II has just passed away: An inspiring and loving leader of the Catholic Church despite my grievances with *some* of both his and the institutions' policies. And one of the many good things he stood for and demonstrated is that the endurance of suffering during human life is part of what defines and gives merit to a truly *authentic* life. (Also, that suffering in others awakens in us the capacity for compassion, one of the highest and most enlightened of human emotions).

Why? How so? I know this may sound like a cheesy platitude and that your parents said it when you were a kid but, apparently, suffering *does* build character. Also sincere, hard, sustained, effort builds character. It just seems to be built in to how things work for the betterment and actualization and affirmation of souls. I think it's Nietche that gets the credit for the term *"what doesn't kill you makes you stronger."* It's the thick-skinned version of the sentiment and it always proves true. Anyone who has endured loss, tragedy or sustained hardship (which winds up being most people, at some point in life) will tell you. We are strengthened by our trials and tribulations and there is an ineffable quality of spiritual maturation that occurs deep within us as well. As initiates to the rite of human experience we acquire (hopefully) some insight into the higher meaning of our lives as we pass through hardship and suffering and grow from them. I think we are growing as spirits, or souls, when we experience compassion for others but this wouldn't be possible if there were no suffering during human life. And this is the authenticity I refer to above: A tested and true, *substance* of character and capacity for love and compassion which are by-products of suffering.

Even romantic love is a form of suffering. We use the word "passion" when we are truly in romantic love, right? Passion literally *means* suffering. Have you ever felt the all consuming passion of really and truly being in love with another human being? There is an almost excruciating longing to spiritually merge, to meld, in a way that utterly transcends sexual union. With this being impossible in the human frame, because our bodies house—and in a way, temporarily "trap"—our souls in our mortal, physical confinement, and keep us separate, it is indeed a form of suffering. Passion hurts.

I think suffering and love are at the very heart of the age old quest for the "meaning of life." I would venture to guess that (for humans, here on Earth) to affirm the existence of love via free will and despite suffering—and the awakening and cultivating of compassion (as in our compassion for Jesus on the cross, which awakens us to our higher spiritual potential), is the meaning and purpose of the sum total of all human experience from time immemorial.

Now, mind you, of course, that these ideas relate to the human experience in the everyday sense and as it applies to individual troubles and hardships, not as concerns natural catastrophes or mans' inhumanity to man. I would never presume to say to victims of the holocaust, child victims of starvation, and victims of earthquakes and tsunami's that their suffering builds character. As far as mans' inhumanity to man is concerned, as I've discussed in previous sections, God doesn't control people's free will. And, as also discussed previously, natural processes are left to their own devices so as to make for an authentic universe.

Chapter 22
But Does All This Mean That God *Never* Communicates with Us in *Any* Way?

When faced with the above question one may jump to one of two immediate conclusions, one: "Of course not, anyone who thinks God is talking to them is either delusional, a megalomaniac, or both." Or, two: "If you pay close and sensitive attention to your life and the people in it, you may realize that God indeed seeks to get your attention in subtle ways." Of course, objectively speaking, there is no way to know the absolute answer to this question. It, like many other branches of the "does God exist?" tree, goes right back to the roots and fundamental matters of faith versus experience.

Having already argued for the existence of God (whether one is Christian or no, my previous support of a God based universe stands on logic: The sum total of existence and everyone in it just doesn't seem possible without original cause), I'd like to address the above question proceeding from the assumption that the God I argue for in this text does indeed exist, and that the question goes once again, back to His nature.

Most people who believe in God, by whatever name or reference, at some point in their lives, feel as though God has abandoned them. The profoundly intense emotions raised by the terrorist attacks of September 11th, 2001 and the Tsunami of Southeast Asia of December 24th, 2004 are two of the most recent examples of how many of the victims and surviving family members may have felt angry at God and abandoned by Him. This may be perceived as an example of the reverse of the above question: God *not* communicating with us (as individuals). And so the question then becomes one of reconciling these things with the idea of the existence of a loving God. As argued in previous sections, for the sake of an authentic universe, we have agreed (I hope) that free will must not be manipulated and neither must the inexorable laws of nature. At such times the faithful, with profound weight of heart and spirit, surrender to and entrust God with tending to absolute Justice in the hope that there is meaning and merit to these tragic events which we cannot now perceive.

But what does it do to my argument when we do indeed sense the opposite? Doesn't it negate the very premise of the case for a God who conforms with the "Prime-Directive"? (a rule from the science fiction mega-hit *Star Trek*, which states that no civilization can be tampered with in such a way so as to alter the course of its natural, social and cultural evolution). It surely would seem to, wouldn't it? But let's not forget what little we *do* seem to know about the nature of God: That while *we*, as humans, are finite, He/She/It is *infinite* and *omniscient*. That would infer that He is infinitely *clever* as well, and that only *He* can figure ways and means of allowing exceptions to his own laws as and when He sees fit. For instance, let's speak briefly of the question of the existence of a*ngels*.

The major three monotheistic religions (Judaism, Christianity and Islam, listed in order of chronological appearance) all draw references to or tell stories about agents of God which act as messengers or intercessors in their sacred texts. We are all familiar with depictions of angels in classical art; winged androgynous beings, mild of manner and hovering above and about us, serving as, if you like, God's field personnel. But what they look like, if they have any *appearance* as we understand the word, at all, scarcely matters. What does matter is that aside from deriving comfort in the belief of their existence, we can recognize them as infinitely loving manifestations of God's "loopholes" in his own laws of existence and non-interference in worldly affairs. Because, it would seem, they are not human and not God, they may be charged with acting as the official trans-dimensional divine operatives.

We read in the Gospels that it was an angel that came to Mary of Nazareth to inform her that she had been chosen to be the vassal of the Christ in what we call "The Annunciation." This wasn't actually an intercession though. However, when she told Joseph, Her betrothed, that she was pregnant, Joseph could hardly be expected to believe that she was pregnant by God. So, the story goes (and it rings true to me, so it's one of the several Gospel accounts I accept literally), an angel came to Joseph (in a dream) and gave him to understand the divine nature of Mary's pregnancy. Also, we have an intercession by angelic council after word gets to the then king of Judea, Herod Antipas, that a "King" has been born. Herod perceives this as a threat to his throne and orders the murder of all infant boys under his jurisdiction. However, as a result of angelic intercession, Mary, Joseph and the infant Jesus escape this grizzly murderous rampage. So, we have Jesus himself being helped by God's messengers, suggesting that were it not for angelic help, Jesus may have been among the victims. Surely, however, the "what kind of God?" question is raised once again at the prospect of rescuing the Christ child but allowing free will to run rampant and deadly upon the lives of those many infants who fell to soldiers' swords.

Is it conceivable then, that on certain occasions for reasons we cannot now perceive that such intercessions (whether we are aware of them or not) take place on behalf of regular folk like you and me. It certainly flies in the face of my contention that the universe would lack authenticity if it were controlled by a cosmic puppeteer. And I still stand by that contention. What kind of God indeed would create a universe based on some cosmic book where everybody's birth, life, behavioral decisions and death have a date and time irrevocably sewn into the fabric of existence? It would be a pointless exercise, and leave no room for merit or meaning. However, at the same time, I must admit that on occasion I am given pause and certain things suggest to me that I may have to allow for exception to (albeit indirectly) God's non-interference pact. It would seem that faith and trust in God is the only way to reconcile this inconsistency. I say this because it would seem that "circumstance" often protects some from fatality when tragedy arises while others meet their end.

Now, according to my argument for the way the universe works, if an anvil falls off a construction site onto your head (forgive the graphic image), it is *not* because *God* did it to you, or that He failed to stop it. He merely conformed to his own laws governing how things *must* be in the course of natural and even tragically accidental events. And it wasn't a matter of marionette strings being manipulated by the Big Cheese in the sky. But can *I,* a telephone cable splicer from the Bronx, claim absolute gnosis and total all encompassing comprehension as to the matrix of existence? Not hardly. Therefore, fully aware of my flawed human condition, but also ever inspired by Socrates' words *"the unexamined life is not worth living,"* on with my query I go, into the quantum like arena of happenstance and the unexplainable.

This became very palpable for me on the fateful morning of September 11th, 2001, especially within the context of my life as a New Yorker in relation to the twin towers of the World Trade Center. I was a little boy in grammar school when the monumental achievement of the two structures was completed. In all the years subsequent to the buildings completion I, like most, was in awe of the two towers and always wanted to go up to the observation deck to see the breathtaking view. I had always heard that the viewer was so high above the ground when taking in the panorama from high atop the towers, that the curvature of the Earth was perceptible to the eye. "One of these days, I gotta go check out that view," I would always say.

But somehow, I never made it a point to make a trip of going into downtown Manhattan and finally getting up to the observation deck. I even worked in the area as a clerk during the early 1990s and would have occasion to deliver a computer tape to a client who would meet me in the lobby of the towers, but I still didn't have occasion to go upstairs so much as one floor.

When hired by the telephone company later, in 1997, I had occasion to pass the World Trade Center often and always marveled at how I had to nearly, literally bend over backwards as I stood on the pavement below in order to see the top, but didn't have occasion to do telephone work on the premises. I worked with several telephone company employees who shared stories of working high on the upper floors and being delighted at the view, even from an upper floor window. But still, neither in my professional nor personal life, did I venture to go up into the buildings.

In 2001 I had been working mostly in midtown Manhattan. But in September of that year I was transferred to "Southern," and would be reporting to 140 West Street, an old "Ma Bell" building across the street from the towers. In the first week or so of working in my new district there was little for my partner and I to do because we were fiber optic cable workers and the necessary equipment for this work had yet to be transferred to the location I was now reporting to. We therefore spent our days of that first week in our new district driving to various locations within the phone company in order to expedite the process of gathering the different supplies we would need in order to get started on jobs. This process was complete by the afternoon of Monday, September 10th, and we were getting rather bored and hoped to be getting started on new jobs soon. The engineering department had drawn up the first work-print for us and we were handed that first job on the morning of 9/11.

Now there were two pieces of this particular job which needed attention. One was at the central office on Pearl Street where service originates and travels along cables through the streets and up into the various subscriber buildings. And the other was at the customer's space, on a high floor of the *North* Tower of the World Trade Center (which would be the first to be struck). My partner and I had a simple choice to make between the hours of 7:30 a.m., when we arrived at work, and 8:47 a.m., the time of first impact by a hijacked airliner. Would we go to the Pearl Street Central office to tend to the first part of the job were our cable originates or proceed directly to the North Tower and begin working on the opposite end of the cable where the service will be provided? I left the decision up to my partner, deferring to his seniority. It was decided that we would review the work-print over a cup of coffee and proceed to the Pearl Street central office. Besides, after the 1993 World Trade Center bombing, special passes would have to be obtained from Pearl Street in order to work at WTC anyway. So, after talking the job over with our boss, and gathering the specific tools and supplies we would need for the job, it was already after 8:00 a.m. After stopping for that all important morning cup of coffee and studying the work-print, we were enroute to Pearl Street on Park Place, about to turn south on Broadway when the deepest, loudest, boom I had ever heard (until fifteen minutes later that is) came from somewhere high above.

The attack had begun. We were ordered by cops to pull the truck aside and let emergency vehicles pass so we were now standing on the sidewalk on Park Row staring in disbelief at the calamity, now an inferno, high above us. It didn't seem like fifteen minutes later, but the minutes passed imperceptibly and the second plane struck the South tower. Any remaining doubts as to the nature of what was transpiring were now gone. In the horror and shock of knowing of the death and devastation taking place up in those buildings, it didn't occur to me until later that day, when I finally got home, that had we decided to go directly up into the North Tower's upper floor to begin our job, we would no doubt have been squarely in the impact zone and lost to this world in an instant.

To this day and for the rest of my life I will grapple with whether this was pure coincidence or something else at work. Unable to know for sure of course, I decided to take the experience as a reminder to take nothing for granted in this life and to make it a priority to try to live up to my potential: To make some sort, however small, of a contribution to the human community, and to value the interactions I have with other human beings as a gift of supreme importance. It's just the underlying emotional and spiritual sense of purpose I personally have taken from such a close call. I must admit it seems as though God does indeed try to convey certain things in subtle ways to us concerning the direction of our lives (I choose the word "try" in this context because I'm convinced that God forces *nothing* on us, receptivity is up to us, I believe). I thought of the deeply moving gospel song featured in the movie adaptation of Alice Walker's *The Color Purple*, called "Maybe God is Tryin' to Tell You Something." In the case of one particular character in the story, the song was meant to serve as a reminder to a woman who had temporarily lost her way that God cares about everybody including those who don't care about God. The larger meaning, it would seem to me, for the song, in and out of the movie, is that we should all try and pay attention if we sense in the smallest, most subtle ways, that maybe God, unworthy and often ungrateful as we are, might be trying to tell us something as we live out our lives trying to make sense of our day to day troubles.

For me, it goes to the heart of the Christian message: that we are never too insignificant for God; that God, in perfect humility, literally (in the form of Christ's life, death and resurrection) and figuratively, leans over to offer us grace and loving guidance but will never force it on us. It is there for the taking should we choose to be open to it. Indeed it goes to the very heart of my inquiry into the nature of God, that although he is no micro-manager, and is rather "hands-off," he wants us to know he is with us nonetheless. He may be silent and imperceptible, and yes, he apparently opts to exercise his divine right to be mysterious, but perhaps that's because what we cannot yet comprehend only *seems* mysterious to us now.

So perhaps, in my personal case, as regards my story of a close call with a sudden death, it wasn't God sending an angel to nudge my partner towards the decision to go to Pearl Street first, but simply coincidence. Does that mean that God wasn't nonetheless trying to tell me something very fundamental about life in general and mine in particular? Coincidence or not, I choose to listen. *I ain't takin' no chances!*

Chapter 23
Holy War: The Original Oxymoron!

When speaking to the idea of being open to God trying to tell us something, it is extremely important for me to be very careful and that's why I chose to include the word "subtle." I don't believe that God communicates with us in overt, visual and/or aural ways. It's more a matter of an individual sensing something that quietly underlies the mundane and which is ineffable, which is detected by what I'd have to describe as extra-sensory perception, that *sixth* sense. There is a danger that when people start believing that God is talking to them in a literal way, or with big, grandiose signs and instructions, that they have some divine mission with categorical prerogative to impose this message on others. Such beliefs are usually the symptoms of those suffering from psychotic conditions such as "delusions of grandeur" or other manifestations of a perceptual break or "split" from reality: Schizophrenia (please do not fall victim to a *hugely popular* misunderstanding and misuse of the word "Schizophrenia." It does *not* mean "split personality"; it means "split from normal sensory perception of reality"). But Schizophrenia doesn't always account for people who insist that God has communicated a definite message to them that must be carried to—and if necessary, imposed upon—others. Oftentimes (altogether *too* often, I'm afraid), it is religious *zeal* that leads to fanaticism in the name of God: A distortion of perception that literally kills.

It kills because religion usually speaks to the idea of absolute reality and what mortals deem to be "God's will." Incendiary emotions can flare out of control because the ego insists that "My way is God's way and everyone else is wrong and *must* be corrected at any cost." This is what gives fuel to the words of Karl Marx, adapted by early communists that religion is the *opiate of the masses.* The idea being that, like a drug, religions can dull the senses or distort them to the point of causing irrational behavior, or both. It leads people to believing that something as horrendous as war can be justified on the grounds of religion alone. There may have, at some point in the history of language, been two words juxtaposed with equal contradiction, but I like to sarcastically refer to the phrase "holy war" as the *original oxymoron* because, to me, no term more clearly gives an example of that description than the profoundly offensive absurdity called "holy war."

For those who hopelessly believe that God is wrathful and vengeful, my words will most likely fall to blind eyes and deaf ears. Wrath and vengeance, for those who choose to mitigate and temper their beliefs and passions with objectivity and intelligence, are *human* emotions. Human = flawed: Divine = Perfect (partly why it's so hard to comprehend the idea of a personified Christ). God, I humbly submit, does *not* suffer from negative human emotions: He is love itself. What kind of God indeed would sanction murder and war in his name? It seems so easy to see the terrible wrong-headed thinking behind waging a "holy war," but it has been a plague of humanity for just about as long as religion has existed.

I will begin with an example from the history of the religion I myself was born into. At around the year 325 of what is now called the "common era" (so as not to impose the Christian calendar or Christian belief on non-Christians), Constantine the Great, a Roman General who rose to the level of Emperor, converted the Roman Empire to Christianity, whereas before it was polytheistic. That much is history. However, on the more legendary side of the story we are told that Constantine (whose mother was a devout Christian: *hint-hint*) had a communication from God on quite a grand scale. The story goes that during the night before the historic battle at the Milvian Bridge, Constantine had a vision. He "saw" a great sign in the sky: Words from God etched into the heavens above him and accompanying the Greek symbol for the Christos (the now common P with an x imposed over the stem of the P) and the words that "appeared" with it were "under this sign will you conquer." And the history of western civilization was forever changed because somebody with great military power was convinced that God sanctioned warfare in the name of Christianity. Now, we can't change history, but this premise was a horrible, twisted distortion of the Christian message and the teachings of Jesus of Nazareth.

Now, mind you, I'm fully aware that I'll be accused of the opposite arrogance: That I think that *I* know what God *doesn't* sanction. Well, my valued reader, I'll just have to take my chances on *that* score, because at least *I* can confidently say that I thoroughly thought through what the nature of a benevolent, loving God might be when it comes to bloodshed and warfare. What kind of God would deem it right and good to slaughter innocent life in the name of faith and belief? What kind of God would condone waging war to force upon others what can only ever be accepted as a matter of conscience and faith? A God with human emotions and human egoism and human will to power, that's what kind. I'm here to humbly submit to you that there is *no such thing as such a god.* And *especially* not one who would take on human form, suffer and die for the purpose of closing the rift between humanity and God. That would be a God of Love, not a God of war or vengeance. This same consternation applies to the whole idea behind the Crusades: That a Pope should decree it as God's will to wage a war to reclaim Jerusalem is yet another fundamental distortion of the basis of Christianity. How do you go from believing in a man that teaches passivity to the point of turning your cheek when struck to offer your offender an undefended chance at striking you again to believing the same guy would instruct you to kill women and children!? There simply is no such thing as a "Holy War," in *any language!* War can *never* be holy, it is living hell. Even when an innocent country is invaded by a hostile neighbor bent on conquest and war becomes necessary, it is a necessary *evil:* A terrible, horrible thing that unfortunately, must be undertaken for the sake of a peoples' right to defend against, for instance, a Hitler type figure: Necessary maybe, but holy, never.

Chapter 24
Religiosity: A Barrier to True Spiritual Experience

It is indeed a very large part of the reason organized religion in *general* has gotten such a bad name by those who criticize and lambaste it as not only *not* a good thing, but an outright *bad* thing. Absolute minded thinking is what leads to the evils of fanaticism, which I've discussed. But so is religiosity when it becomes a wall. Joseph Campbell, a great scholar of world myths and comparative religion, in his book *The Power of Myth* cites religiosity as the final barrier to the true religious experience. I couldn't agree more. What happens is that people get caught up in the rituals and practices, pomp and circumstance, and general formalities and even symbols and imagery of their formal mode of worship to the point where these things *become* the religious experience instead of being things that guide or enhance the religious experience or the feeling of closeness with God. And so, ironically, that which may have genuinely been *intended* to *facilitate* an experience of high spirituality ultimately serves to block a more real and authentic sense of communion with God. And speaking of "communion," therein lays a good example to illustrate my point.

In the Catholic Mass, the festivities are concluded by the congregation (those who "qualify" by rite of Catholic doctrine and Canon) being served small wafers of bread to commemorate (by Jesus' request per scripture) not only the last supper, but the sacrifice that Jesus made with his body and his human life via the Passion for the sake of all humankind. *So the bread represents his body.* Now, to many, my preceding sentence either borderlines sacrilege or is outright sacrilegious.

Debates have *raged* over the centuries and schisms caused by what this bread either is, or isn't, literally or figuratively. I recall being "told" that a "transmutation" takes place, that Christ figuratively turns the host (the wafer) into his "body" by virtue of the Holy Spirit changing the nature of the bread by his blessing upon it and his presence *in* it. Then, later, I was "corrected" and "told" that indeed an outright (and you're going to love this word) *trans-substantiation* occurs. That this bread isn't just blessed or become a vessel through which one may commune with the Holy Spirit, the less tangible, more abstract Godhead, but has literally, concretely, absolutely and *physically* been turned into the *flesh* of Jesus. Now for goodness sake, if anything serves to block the communal experience of Christianity it's this nonsense. We can get so caught up in the nature of the wafer and the physical nature of the Eucharist that we lose the sense of communion with Jesus that *can* come with prayerful meditation and openness to the love that this remembrance *embodies*. Jesus himself (and of course we must realize, that Jesus' words and quotes are a slippery slope, the Gospels aren't consistent and were subject to multiple translations over the centuries—and we have to sort of go with our gut feeling regarding what may have been enhanced, added, deleted or translated inaccurately, usually for reasons of controlling the masses during the dark ages) was religiously revolutionary if for nothing else but to remind the Jews of his day (and anyone in his part of the world that would listen) that the *letter* of the law shouldn't be the ultimate focus, but the living heart and essence should. And if anybody proved that such a living heart and essence is an organic thing that changes and evolves and must never be stagnant or concretized into inflexible fundamentalist literalism regarding religion, it was Jesus of Nazareth. So let us beware of the bells and whistles of religiosity and simply try to tune into the underlying silence through which God just may be *communing* with *us*.

Usually, the times when the "God question" is most sorely put to the test, or indeed comes up at all, are the times when our experience or observations make belief in an absolute "Good" run counterintuitive to what our senses process, i.e. war, hatred, tragedy and all the things that raise our ire at the very notion of God. But how often, I wonder, do we *experience* God without an *equal and opposite reaction* in the processing of our senses that at least *whispers* to us, that indeed God is there? I'm tempted to compare it to the phenomenon of bad news being what sells newspapers. We read of the bad and *it's* what registers. We don't read about senseless acts of random kindness, they don't *move units*, we read about random acts of senseless vicious violence: It sells, and it gets television ratings.

And so it goes with the God question. We don't seem to shake our tightly clenched fists at the sky—when:

* We see a sunset that casts a million fingers of perfectly complimenting pastel colors swirling around the horizon, quietly creating within us a sense of peace and tranquility that is utterly sublime.

* We see a new mother cradling in her arms a brand new life that didn't exist in this world just nine months previous (three times three, by the way).

* A person dives into a freezing river to save the life of a perfect stranger.

* Flowers bloom and trees blossom each and every spring *all by themselves.*

* A piece of music moves a person so deeply inside that they are given to weeping.

* A person has a voice for singing with such a magical and unique, beautiful *sound* to it, that we can't contain our emotional reaction.

* We experience the awesome power of love; the love that raises us up and out of ourselves and reminds us that we are but a part of something far bigger than any one individual.

* We see photos of the Earth from space, so beautiful and teeming with life in an otherwise lifeless solar system.

* We look up at the night sky, far from obtrusive city lights, and contemplate the beauty of the stars and the seeming infinitude of the universe, and wonder: "is there anyone *else— anywhere—*out there?

* When a stranger holds a door open simply because it was a nice thing to do.

* When we feel the indescribable power of receiving or offering forgiveness or compassion.

* When we know, first hand, what it is to be truly loved.

I humbly submit, that I think we *experience* God more than we often realize.

Chapter 25
And What *About* That Question of "Is There Anybody *Out* There?"

A *truly open mind*, one that is free of fundamentalist programming or fear of universality, is prepared to consider the God question in a far broader context than our Earth bound one. How is the God question or our perspective on the existence of God affected by the idea of sentient life existing elsewhere, somewhere in the unimaginable vastness of the universe? Our own Galaxy, the Milky Way may well be teeming with life. But inconceivably, incomprehensibly, enormously vast pinwheels of stars (a simple definition of what a "galaxy" is) exist out there in what astronomers call "clusters." So, approaching the question from the scientific point of view that says "if conditions are right, life will emerge and evolve," we are faced with the very real possibility of not being the only self-aware species in the grand cosmic picture.

Before Galileo, the Catholic Church dictated that the Earth was the center of the universe; a *geocentric* perspective. Thanks to Galileo, however, and hard scientific methodology, we now know that, first of all, we are not talking about the *entire* cosmos, but only our local star system, our solar system, and that indeed *that* particular star, our Sun, is at the center of the orbital schema, and that *we* rotate around *it:* A heliocentric *realization.* Well, this historical fact seems to have a modern day parallel. Instead of being convinced of a *geocentric* perspective, many people (usually religious fundamentalists, for a change, from *any* religion that puts the *kabash* on free thinking) stubbornly maintain an *anthropocentric* perspective on the universe; one that is seemingly incapable of imagining anything but human beings at the center of all existence. Of course the important difference in the parallel I draw is that, as yet, neither science nor extraterrestrial beings have confirmed, proof positive, that sentient life exists elsewhere or *else-when* in the universe.

Why is the very notion such an intellectual "bogey-man" to the religious fundamentalist? I think because it upsets their little neat and tidy, narrow minded view of human life and its place in the universe. Maybe the perceived threat is not dissimilar, as regards the God and man equation, to the toddler who perceives his or her newborn sibling to be a threat to the love and affection status with the parent; in short, they want to be God's *only,* not just his favorite.

When contemplated objectively, however, the God question, in the broad sense, isn't really changed at all by the idea that there could be soul-inhabited, sentient beings somewhere in existence besides the Earth. On a cosmic scale it is equivalent to there being many bodies of land separated by massive bodies of water here on Earth and inhabited by many different groups of people with different world-views; most of whom where not aware of the others' existence before maritime technology afforded seafaring voyages of discovery. In fact we need to spiritually and intellectually evolve to the point of transcending the xenophobia so pervasive here on Earth before we can even-handedly cope with "the different" from entirely *other* worlds, because God *may* have many other children than we are comfortable with accepting.

One may ask, however: Since this book clearly argues not only for the existence of a personal and loving God, but argues for a God that participated not only in life here in the physical universe in general, but in *humanity* in particular (a decidedly Christian perspective I totally acknowledge), where does such open-mindedness leave the *Jesus question?* I'll tell you where: Out there on a limb called "faith," where it was in the first place! I used to be convinced that discovery of extraterrestrial-sentient life would all but entirely *squash* the Jesus question as utterly and irreconcilably anthropocentric cosmic debris. Because it would mean that God personified *here*, and went through life, love, death and resurrection *here*, on *Earth*, without regard for God's children elsewhere in the universe. Well, I'm not so sure of that anymore. Sure, the Jesus question is faced with new challenges as far as reconciling it to reason as I need to do, but I need to do that here on the *terrestrial* scene as well. Jesus lived in a place and time where whole peoples on the other side of the Globe had no way of knowing that he walked among us. Did that, by itself, diminish the reality of his walking? No, I submit, It didn't, it couldn't, it doesn't, and it wont: It can't.

Would that mean then, that future space-faring Earthlings would have a cosmic mandate to go out into other star systems converting cosmic pagans to Christianity like some twenty-fourth century (just a guess) conquistador?: Absolutely not. Nobody *ever* had a right to force Christianity on *any* people. Let those who feel they should "preach the word" do so, if proselytizing *(peacefully and non-judgmentally!)* is what they want to do. But if you want to share your beliefs with others, maybe getting on a cosmic soap box isn't the best way to go about it. Perhaps simply writing them down and hoping for publication in the *Milky Way Times* might do it. A good soul in an interstellar library somewhere out in the Seven Sisters constellation just might pick it up and browse through it! Hey, you never know.

Chapter 26
The Ultimate "What If" Scenario

For those of us unencumbered by religious indoctrination (people-programming), and/or xenophobia, who enjoy the freedom of thought which an independent, self-reliant, intellectually liberated individual mind has a responsibility to itself to indulge, contemplation of the very real possibility (indeed, according to many astronomers, likelihood) of there being life elsewhere in the universe comes naturally and is accepted readily. We accept the challenge that it poses to our perception of whom and what we are in the grand cosmic scheme of things. We invite it into our general query as to the nature of God despite how thought provoking and even intimidating a thing it is.

I believe it intimidates us because it forces us to ponder the staggering vastness of space and the fact that the more one does so, the more insignificant one tends to begin to feel. But if we are secure in our sense of identity and know that we are precious individuals, each one of us, we can be comfortable with the prospect of God having created many families of sentient life, scattered throughout the incomprehensible infinitude of the universe.

But if we are to remain true to an honest, objective, intellectually responsible weighing of the cosmic scale, than philosophical integrity demands that we contemplate one more mentally and emotionally challenging proposition, perhaps the ultimate "what if" scenario: What if God did indeed create the universe, and, as argued earlier, left it to its own devices so as not to play cosmic puppeteer, but because of the infinitude of combinations of chance and conditions, and the miraculous quantum leap required to *go* from those conditions and combinations to the building blocks of life; those first organic molecules swimming in the primordial soup that would play host to evolution, it just so happened to turn out that the recipe for life came together here, but *only* here? Yes, we owe it to ourselves and to honesty to be equally as opened minded about *this* possible scenario as we are of the sentient life form containing, extra-terrestrial one. We don't know which one is the case right now, so we *must* consider both.

I *sub*mit as well as *ad*mit that there is a bit of a sentimental, if albeit anthropocentric, dimension to this reverse cosmic scenario. I say so because, as we take our imaginative journey outward toward the stars in *this* thought experiment, and race, at light speed in our minds eye, long after the Earth has quickly receded to the size of a pin and then vanished in our rear view mirror. And long after our own solar system has melted into the background of a myriad of stars like a single grain of sand is lost in the Sahara desert, and than after our great speed dwarfs our own Milky Way galaxy into memory as it too, shows itself to be, in our faster than light space craft, an untraceable pinwheel of stars buried in cluster after cluster of galaxies, after nebula and black hole alike, are but a blur to our overwhelmed eyes, and not a trace of life is to be found, we begin *not* to feel insignificant at all, but are overwhelmed with just how significant we really *are*.

The enormity of our value as human beings comes rushing down upon us and all around us and fills us with an overpowering desire to get back to our precious, miraculous little blue green world, despite the beauty and wonder of the vast cosmos, to tell our family and friends how much we love them and how infinitely important they are to us and to the very affirmation of the existence of life in this or *any* dimension. Because, at the end of the day, it is *we* who bring merit and meaning to life, alone in the universe or not. It falls to *us* to realize that love through free will, and growth through great struggle, is the reason for our existence.

The sum total of all human experience will show, in the final culmination of *all that is*, that *we* not only did well to believe in *God,* but that *God* did well to believe in *us*.

May peace be with you no matter what your religion is or your conception of the nature of reality. And thank you for reading my little book.

Printed in the United States
74979LV00002B/8

9 781424 152360